AN APPROACH TO

MEASURING RESULTS IN SOCIAL WORK

AN APPROACH TO

MEASURING RESULTS IN SOCIAL WORK

A Report on the
Michigan Reconnaissance Study of
Evaluative Research in Social Work
Sponsored by the Michigan Welfare League

BY DAVID G. FRENCH

With Analyses of
Four Evaluative Studies prepared by
JOHN G. HILL, LEON FESTINGER
HELEN L. WITMER *and* ALFRED J. KAHN

GREENWOOD PRESS, PUBLISHERS
WESTPORT, CONNECTICUT

THIS STUDY WAS MADE POSSIBLE THROUGH THE GENEROSITY
OF THE JAMES FOSTER FOUNDATION OF ANN ARBOR, MICHIGAN

PREFACE

WHEN A PERSON interested in the welfare of others looks at the entire picture of social work, he is impressed with two things. First, the size of the job; second, the lack of real knowledge regarding its effectiveness.

In Michigan alone, the annual expenditure of voluntary funds for social work is between $15 and $20 million and public expenditures are well over $100 million. The total is estimated to come to more than $125 million per year.

If these were industrial expenditures, they would be guided by a sizable staff of research scientists. Modifications and improvements have always resulted from such scientific industrial research. Can we not expect similar results from scientific research in social work?

Mr. French, through his studies and in his book, has suggested ways and means of strengthening scientific research in the programs of operating social work organizations and of graduate schools of social work. His book is directed primarily toward social work in Michigan, but, even in this study, he found it necessary to go far beyond the boundaries of one state for experience and persons with knowledge of research in social work. The report of this study will be of interest to people in any state.

I must repeat what Mr. French states in his Foreword: "This is *not* a piece of evaluative research." It is a reconnaissance. It points out some of the places where successful research may be expected; where it is doubtful of success; and where it certainly will not succeed, at least with our present knowledge of how to conduct research in social work. It draws a map, a map with particular reference to Michigan, it is true, but the map may easily be modified to fit other states. The study suggests a plan of attack. It describes ways and means for implementing the attack, and then, with a true researcher's viewpoint, Mr. French suggests the attack be carried on simultaneously by several independent researchers.

The Michigan Welfare League sponsored this reconnaissance study. The League is a state-wide planning organization. It works with both private agencies and tax-supported agencies. It is in a unique position to provide continuing stimulation for more and better research in social work. The Board of the League outlined the idea of a reconnaissance study; they secured the financial support necessary from the James Foster Foundation and located in Mr. French an outstanding person to conduct such a study.

The pattern for effective evaluative research which is outlined in this book was unknowingly used in miniature in the organization of the reconnaissance study. Here was a social work agency, the League, employing a research person, Mr. French, and supported in its project by a foundation, the James Foster Foundation. The team worked well. Each supported the other. The result is a valuable step toward sound, basic research in social work.

FRANKLIN W. WALLIN
President, Michigan Welfare League

Jenison, Michigan
August, 1952

FOREWORD

DURING THE SUMMER of 1950 the Board of Directors of the Michigan Welfare League conceived the idea of the Michigan Reconnaissance Study of Evaluative Research in Social Work. Members of the Board, approximately two-thirds of them laymen in the field of social work and one-third of them employed professionally in the field, were concerned about certain questions which were put to them repeatedly in one form or another by their friends and associates: Are people being benefited by social work services in the way they need to be benefited? Is the money which the community is investing in social work services producing results which justify continuing or extending these services? What kinds of improvement are possible in making social work services more effective?

Rather than launch into a research project which would try to get specific answers to these questions in one or two social work programs, the Board decided first to survey some of the past attempts to evaluate social work services, to identify the obstacles which had been encountered, and to explore the possibilities for developing a continuing research program in social work which would be able to provide some answers as to the effectiveness of particular social work services.

The interest of the Michigan Welfare League Board coincided with that of the National Board of the American Association of Social Workers, which, particularly during the past five years, has devoted a substantial portion of its resources to stimulating research in social work. The National Board of the Association was therefore glad to accede to the request of the

Michigan Welfare League for a leave of absence for the author to work with the League on the proposed project.

It is important to stress that this study has been a *reconnaissance* study on evaluative research. It is *not* a piece of evaluative research. It has been carried on with specific reference to the problems and the resources of social work in Michigan. Its analysis and general recommendations, however, are intended to have general applicability to the field of social work and it is hoped they will contribute to the discussions going forward on the use of research in social work programs.

It has not been possible in the course of this study to review all the research efforts which merited review and to delve into their successes and failures, or to solicit the counsel of all the persons in social work and in related fields whose experience and observations could contribute to the recommendations of this study. Every exploratory study of this kind reaches a cut-off point which is dictated not by a sense of completion of the project but by the calendar. In a sense, this report is a progress report. It is hoped that others will be stimulated to test and to confirm or correct the analysis and recommendations presented.

I would like to express my appreciation here for the suggestions and criticisms which the members of the Advisory Committee to the study have contributed as the study progressed. I am indebted also to numerous other people who have discussed various aspects of the project and participated in the conferences arranged by the Reconnaissance Study. Special appreciation is due the four consultants who prepared the analyses of evaluative research projects which are reproduced in Appendix B: Mr. John G. Hill, Dr. Helen L. Witmer, Dr. Alfred J. Kahn, and Dr. Leon Festinger; to the participants who took part in a two-day conference in New York City on the relationship of social science and social work research: Miss Anne Geddes, Dr. Robert Merton, Dr. Norman Polansky, Dr. Christopher Sower, Mr. Stephen Withey, Dr. Helen Witmer, and Dr. Donald Young; and to the practitioners, administrators, and board members who took part in three conferences in Michigan to identify problems for evaluative research in social work and whose names are listed in Appendix A in connection with the conferences they attended.

I am happy to express my personal appreciation and that of the Reconnaissance Study to Dr. Rensis Likert and the Institute for Social Research at the University of Michigan for providing office space for the Study and for the informal consultations which members of the Institute contributed while the study was in process.

I am glad also to express my appreciation to members of the National Board of The American Association of Social Workers and to the Association's executive secretary, Mr. Joseph Anderson, for their willingness to adjust a very full Association program to make possible a leave of absence for the conduct of this study.

Finally, I should like to express my appreciation to the Board of Directors of the James Foster Foundation for the grant which made this study possible and for their interest and encouragement throughout the planning and conduct of the study.

DAVID G. FRENCH

Ann Arbor, Michigan
September, 1952

CONTENTS

xiv *Contents*

AN APPROACH TO

MEASURING RESULTS
IN SOCIAL WORK

CHAPTER I

THE REASON FOR THE STUDY

PEOPLE ARE ASKING FOR RESEARCH

Three groups of people, at least, have been expressing concern about research in social work. First among them are the "lay" members of social agency boards and of community chests and councils. This group is important for a number of reasons, not least of which is that it holds the purse strings. Every year hundreds of thousands of dollars in Michigan pass through the hands of budget committee members of community chests, and millions of dollars are allocated by members of the state legislature—all "laymen" in the field of social work. If research efforts in social work are going to receive the kind of support they require, the laymen are going to have to understand and back those efforts.

The second group concerned about research in social work is made up of the men and women who are "professionals." One social worker in writing to the program committee of the National Conference of Social Work in 1951 expressed the widespread feeling of this group in these words: "We social workers have real conviction about the value of what we do, both to the client and community. But can we prove it? Is it possible to prove it? By what methods? Many of us are dissatisfied with the traditional research methods for establishing that social work service is or is not, at the present time, the best possible way of dealing with certain problems. But what methods *would* establish, both for the public and for us, the value—and I mean the unique value—in what we are doing? . . . It's a difficult problem—that of discovering the research method appropriate for evaluating the efficacy of social work as a method—but it is one I would like to see worked on." [1] Declarations of this kind are legion.

The social scientists comprise the third group. Fundamental research in human behavior and in human relations is the job of social scientists. Evidence of their interest in tackling research problems in social work is found in the concluding statement of Donald Young's first annual report as General Director of the Russell Sage Foundation, written shortly after he retired as President of the Social Science Research Council. "As the Foundation sees the situation," he wrote, "Both social science and social practice have made great advances in recent decades, but as they have progressed there has been costly failure by each to maintain sufficiently close liaison with the other. Research needs to be kept realistic by contact with the practitioners who use its results; the practitioners need to keep informed about the frontiers of research knowledge bearing on their techniques. Responsibility for the current lack of adequate attention to this fact lies not chiefly with either the social scientists or the practitioners. . . . The problem seems to be that it has been almost no one's accepted responsibility to develop and maintain the needed liaison." [2] Emphasis on the importance of relating scientific research to the everyday problems of our social order is characteristic of social scientists today.

With the three groups most immediately concerned in such unanimous agreement that research in social work is needed, and especially evaluative research, it should be possible to get

[1] Joint Committee on Program Planning, National Conference of Social Work and the National Social Welfare Assembly, Memorandum of April 27, 1951 (Columbus: National Conference of Social Work, 1951; mimeograph).
[2] Russell Sage Foundation, *Annual Report 1947–48* (New York: Russell Sage Foundation, 1948), p. 14.

some practical research efforts under way. This study has been conducted with that goal in mind.

During the course of the study the attitude was frequently encountered, particularly among administrators and professional practitioners, that we already know more than we are putting to use in social work programs. Not new knowledge, but use of existing knowledge, is the first order of the day, they asserted. Two illustrations are worth recording.

In 1949, the Detroit Department of Public Welfare was being investigated by a committee in the City Controller's Office. A subcommittee on case reading, after sampling the records, produced the following statistics, among other data: [3]

The average case in the department had been handled by four different workers.

The average length of time during which each worker carried a case was four months.

The average number of contacts (home or office) between worker and client was slightly over one per month.

Two-thirds of the caseworkers carrying cases at the time of the study had no professional social work training whatever.

Over against this kind of service, which was the best that the agency was able to provide, the array of problems in the cases under scrutiny seems rather overwhelming: In addition to the economic problem which occasioned the need for fi-

[3] Detroit, Michigan, City Controller's Office, Committee Inquiring into the Department of Public Welfare, *Report of Sub-Committee on Case Reading* (February, 1949; mimeograph), p. 58.

nancial assistance, workers reported health problems in 65 percent of the family cases, problems of family relationships in 59 percent of the cases, and personality and behavior disorders in 42 percent of the cases. The incidence of health problems in the one-person cases amounted to 83 percent.

Public welfare workers already know certain measures that would improve the program of the Detroit Welfare Department without resort to time-consuming and expensive research: smaller case loads, less staff turnover, better supervision to assure appropriate use of all community resources on the difficult cases. But putting such measures into effect should not be regarded as an alternative to tackling the basic questions which trouble people who think about our assistance programs: why some people go on relief and others do not; what methods of providing assistance strengthen the self-reliance and initiative of people, while others sap these qualities; and what preventive measures might be instituted to reduce the number of people who have to apply for assistance. The choice is not action *or* research, but action *and* research.

The second illustration of our failure to use existing knowledge comes from a vocational school for delinquent boys. In discussing this school, a prominent social worker stated that he does not need research to tell him what is needed: namely, another institution. As long as all kinds of children are put in one place, the institution has to be run to fit five percent of the boys. Furthermore, pressure for space makes it necessary to discharge boys too early. Because the school is no larger than it was when the state had half so many people, the obvious step is to build another institution.

In a sense, this social worker is right. But should there be two, or perhaps six, small institutions? How are the boys to be classified appropriately for different kinds of institutional treatment? What about testing the results of premature discharge?

What about the soundness of any program which returns a boy to the same situation in which his delinquency developed? When these questions were raised, it was necessary to admit that they could not be answered in time for the coming session of the legislature. But it was pointed out that research might provide a basis for sound action ten years hence. The social worker was not easily swayed. His comment was, "I hope we don't have to wait that long to get a second institution."

Actually there is not so much conflict between a research and a common-sense approach as the above illustration suggests. Agency executives and commissions cannot wait until all the answers are in before making decisions about their programs for this month or next year. Surveys like that made of the Detroit Welfare Department, or like the one made of the Boys' Vocational School in 1946, and never acted on, are important and necessary. But if surveys and studies remain always on this level our progress will be terribly painful and slow. Engineers did not try to design the electric iron until they had a pretty good idea of the way electricity behaved. Yet in social work we are confronted with the necessity of devising and operating far more complicated social mechanisms without any solid grasp of the forces being dealt with.

CAUTION: DON'T EXPECT TOO MUCH

At one point in the Reconnaissance Study a small group of social scientists and research specialists in social work came together to review some of the recommendations being prepared for this report. On one point there was complete unanimity: don't oversell research. Dr. Robert Merton of Columbia University said it this way:

There is one danger that needs special attention in an affair of this kind: that of overstating the claims regarding what social research will do for social work. This takes one form above all others, and that is not having an adequate time perspective. I have the impression that this undertaking is being considered with the idea that, in the space of a few years, five perhaps, there will be a very notable impact of social research on practice in social work. As a personal view I think this is very unlikely, for the reason that when we come down to discussing any particular piece of research, it is highly unlikely one could mobilize the enormous resources that would be needed to make any impact in terms of five years or so.

There is a very special reason for making this warning more than a pious suggestion. One of the dangers to which every new kind of applied social research is subject is the quick disillusionment of the group that has become enamored of the idea. Moreover, some social researchers are guilty of provoking the disillusionment by making overclaims that they feel are necessary in order to get an opening wedge.

More typically, it is the research consumer, rather than the researcher, who is apt to have exaggerated notions of the benefits of research. One man, who had made a number of studies for industrial plants, commented, "When a piece of research on a limited problem is carried through successfully it tends to be overaccepted, particularly if the conclusions coincide with the views of a vice president in the company. The implications of that little piece of research are blown up to such gargantuan dimensions that the hair of the researcher stands on end—permanently." Regardless of the source of the overexpectation, if research consumers start off with hopes that have not been toned down appropriately, there is bound to be disillusionment.

There are two ways of taking this word of warning not to expect too much from research in the very near future. One is to give up any vigorous pursuit of evaluative research and to rely on the best hunches and estimates we can muster. The other is to accept the fact that it will be some time before tangible and practical results can be expected of evaluative research efforts in social work, but to work hard now to get the basic research under way which will make possible useful and productive evaluative research some years hence.

Social work has been described as operating on the crisis theory, with a new crisis to contend with every hour on the hour. Social work *has* been under the necessity of taking practical steps to deal with the various crises that have emerged in the years of depression and war in which we have been living. Today's need has been so pressing that there has been little energy or interest left for examining the consequences of yesterday's acts. This is understandable, but it does not mean that it must be accepted as the normal and appropriate path for the development of social work as a profession. One of the phrases heard frequently at the 1951 National Conference of Social Work was "social work's coming to maturity." A sign of social work's maturity will be the ability to meet the new crises of tomorrow while at the same time providing for the patient, slow, but steady building up of a body of social work knowledge that has been tested and substantiated.

THE APPROACH OF THE RECONNAISSANCE STUDY

The approach of the Reconnaissance Study is reflected in the organization of the material in this report. Chapter II summarizes the over-all investment which the people of Michigan are making in social work. Chapter III brings together some of the questions which both professional and lay persons are asking about social work and considers the implications of these questions for planning a research program. Chapter IV analyzes what is involved in doing evaluative research; reviews some representative studies to determine in what respects they were successful and in what respects they fell short; and examines the implications of their experience for evaluative research in social work.

Chapter V considers the relationship between scientific research and research in a field of practice as a basis for planning a research program in social work. Chapter VI establishes criteria for a continuing program of research in social work and considers the appropriate administrative setting for such research. Chapter VII makes suggestions concerning the launching of an institute for research in social work in Michigan.

PROCEDURE IN THE STUDY

A variety of procedures have been used in carrying out the Reconnaissance Study. First, certain factual information about social work and about research has been assembled which has a bearing on the planning of a research program in social work. Secondly, as much of the literature as possible was reviewed dealing with the general problem of applied research and particularly with social science research and social work. Thirdly, both individual and group conferences were held to solicit information that was not readily available in printed form, to get suggestions and observations about the conduct of evaluative research in social work, and to test out portions of the analysis and the conclusions developed during the course of the study. The final report draws heavily on all of these sources, more than it has been possible to indicate with specific footnote references. Final responsibility for what is presented, of course, rests with the author.

Before proceeding with the body of the report it may help the reader to call attention now to a shift in focus which occurred early in the study. As the study went forward, the emphasis shifted from evaluation to research. It became clear that the minute one undertakes research to evaluate a practice or a policy one encounters the basic problems of classification, of design, of measurement which plague any kind of scientific research. The lack of more adequate evaluative research in social work in the past is not due to a dearth of people to ask, "How well are we doing?" but to the fact that these basic problems of research in human behavior have proved so difficult.

The evaluative interest is retained, however, and for a definite reason. It is perhaps the most strategic point at which to bring together the practical concerns of the social worker and the more theoretical concerns of the researcher. Kurt Lewin, one of the most discerning students of man and his institutions, wrote: "If we cannot judge whether an action has led forward or backward, if we have no criteria for evaluating the relation between effort and achievement, there is nothing to prevent us from making the wrong conclusions and to encourage the wrong work habits. Realistic fact finding and evaluation is a prerequisite for any learning." [4]

It is hard to ignore Kurt Lewin's logic; it led him, as it will lead anyone, back to the basic problems in the scientific study of man.

[4] Kurt Lewin, "Frontiers in Group Dynamics," *Human Relations*, I, No. 2 (1947), p. 150.

CHAPTER II

THE COMMUNITY'S INVESTMENT IN SOCIAL WORK

SOCIAL WORK is big business in two respects: it costs a great deal of money and it affects a great number of people. Social work's growth to its present size is recent, the bulk of it occurring during the past twenty-five years. This helps account for the fact that many people are not aware of the role this field of activity has come to play in community and national life. One university official expressed amazement when told that expenditures for social work services in Michigan alone amounted to over $125 million per year and asked, "How is it that one who has been involved in social research as much as I have been over the last twenty years could have been exposed so little to what goes on in social work?"

One answer is that graduate professional schools of social work are relatively late comers to most university campuses and are still not completely part of the university community in many places. Another answer is that there is little material in the general undergraduate curriculum of the university which deals with social work concepts and programs. As Ernest Hollis has pointed out in his recent study of social work education, the absence of such material has resulted in "the production of a generation of city and county officials, legislators, governors, educators, doctors, businessmen, lawyers, labor leaders, and citizens in hundreds of other occupations who do not have enough understanding of the purpose and operation of public and private welfare programs to give them the support commonly accorded health and education activities." [1]

Today Michigan has three graduate schools of social work located at its three large universities. There are some 3,500 persons employed full time in social work positions. Every city of 30,000 population or more has its community chest, and every one of the eighty-three counties has its Department of Social Welfare. Six departments of state government are engaged in providing social work services as part of their programs. The department which is primarily engaged in social work, the Michigan Department of Social Welfare, is matched only by the Highway Department and the Department of Public Instruction in the size of its budget and the number of persons it employs.

There is no need to labor further the significant place which social work has come to occupy in both voluntary community enterprise and in government. The only purpose in underscoring this situation at the beginning of the report is to bring out the tremendous stake which the people of Michigan and of all the other states have in effective planning and carrying out of social services.

WHAT IS INCLUDED IN SOCIAL WORK

For the purpose of getting a broad picture of the money involved in and the people affected by social work there is no need to grapple with the difficult question of the precise boundaries of social work. We have at hand a working definition of the field which was used by the Bureau of Labor Statistics of the United States Department of Labor in its 1950 survey of social work personnel in the United States. The same

[1] Ernest V. Hollis and Alice L. Taylor, *Social Work Education in the United States* (New York: Columbia University Press, 1951), p. 162.

definition has been used in this report. Its virtue is that it specifies the particular programs and personnel which are considered to be within social work for the purposes of that survey, and anyone wishing to use a narrower definition can adjust the figures accordingly.[2] The following figures are taken from a pilot survey to the national survey which was conducted in Michigan in November, 1948. They show more detail for this state than do the national figures.

Table 1. Distribution of Social Workers among Programs in Michigan, 1948

Type of Program	Percent of All Workers
Public assistance	35
Family service other than public assistance	9
Child welfare work	9
Court services for children	5
School social work	3
Social work in mental hygiene clinics	1
Social work in mental hospitals	3
Social work in medical hospitals and clinics	3
Social work with adult offenders	6
Veterans' counseling and assistance	4
Other services to families and individuals	5
Group work—building-centered programs	8
Group work—non-building–centered programs	5
Community organization work	3
Teaching social work	1
Total	100

Source: Lily Mary David, "Social Work Salaries and Working Conditions in Michigan," *Social Work Journal,* XXX, No. 2 (April, 1949), p. 64.

[2] For a detailed list of positions classified as falling within social work see *Social Workers in 1950,* A Report on the Study of Salaries and Working Conditions in Social Work, made by the Bureau of Labor Statistics, United States Department of Labor (New York: American Association of Social Workers, 1952), p. 28.

Such programs as public housing and social insurance are omitted from Table 1, although a case can be made for including them in a broad definition of social work. At the present time these programs do not look to the field of social work as a major source of personnel, nor do the schools of social work offer special training for work in these programs. Nevertheless, many of the problems being dealt with in these programs are hardly distinguishable from those encountered in social work programs as defined in the Bureau of Labor Statistics survey.

It should be noted also that Table 1 excludes the health programs which are supported by community chests. Health and welfare services are frequently bracketed in the public's mind because the annual Red Feather drives that are carried on throughout the country seek funds for both types of services in a single package. Since this report is concerned with research in social work, the health programs are excluded from the figures presented, except for the social work units of health programs, such as the medical social work departments of hospitals.

The distribution of personnel among social work programs shown in Table 1 provides some indication of the relative size of these programs. It does not, of course, indicate the distribution of expenditures among them. Public assistance, since its primary service is making financial grants to eligible persons, accounts for over 80 percent of social work expenditures, although it employs only 35 percent of the social workers.

EXPENDITURES FOR SOCIAL WORK SERVICES

Funds for carrying on social work programs come from three sources: taxes, voluntary contributions, and fees for service. The first source is much the largest, in Michigan providing approximately 85 percent of the money which goes into social work programs. Of this 85 percent, over nine-tenths is spent for financial assistance to the aged, the blind, the handicapped, dependent children, and other needy persons. Less than one-tenth of the money going into publicly financed social work programs goes to support activities which are not related to assistance. Thus while public expenditures loom large in relation to expenditures from voluntary sources, when the financial assistance programs are omitted as much or more money is spent on voluntary social work services as on social work services financed through taxes.

The personnel figures compiled by the Bureau of Labor Statistics in its 1948 pilot survey of social workers in Michigan bear out the relative size of public and voluntary social work programs. That survey showed that of the 3,492 full-time social workers in Michigan in November, 1948, 1,240, or 36 percent, were employed in public assistance, 1,057, or 30 percent, in other tax-supported agencies, and 1,195, or 34 percent, in voluntary agencies. Both the expenditure and personnel figures indicate that, excluding the field of public assistance, there is somewhat more money and personnel involved in voluntary social work programs than in tax-supported programs. This fact has particular significance when we consider later in this report the financing of research in social work.

Complete figures on expenditures for social work programs in even a single state such as Michigan are not available, and on a nation-wide basis only the most general estimates can be obtained. One recent study estimated a $2.5 billion annual expenditure for social work services, using a definition of social work similar to that used in the Bureau of Labor Statistics survey.[3] In Michigan, a fair estimate of total 1950 expenditures in social work programs as defined by the Bureau of Labor Statistics would be in the neighborhood of $125 million, of which roughly 85 percent was derived from taxes, 11 percent

[3] Hollis and Taylor, *op. cit.*, p. 65.

from voluntary contributions, and 4 percent from payments by users of the services. The largest proportion of the last amount was paid by persons using the building-centered group work agencies, which derive a substantial income from membership fees, cafeteria operations, etc.

Tables 2 and 3 show expenditures in 1950 by voluntary agencies affiliated with community chests in cities with 50,000 population or more and by departments of the state government. The tables do not include expenditures by the American Red Cross, which amounted to over $500 thousand in 1950, or expenditures by city and county governments. It is known that in the field of foster care for children alone over $2 million was spent by county governments in the year 1949.[4] However, the tables bring together the readily available information on

Table 2. Expenditures by Social Work Agencies Affiliated with Community Chests in Michigan, 1950 [a]

Type of Program	Expenditures	Percent of Total
Family service	$ 1,677,641	11
Child welfare	3,739,431	25
Group work and leisure time	8,276,901	56
Services for the aged	180,700	1
Services for the handicapped	187,882	1
Psychiatric clinics	94,658	1
Community planning and fund raising	792,609	5
Total	$14,949,822	100

[a] Figures from community chests in all cities of Michigan with a population of 50,000 or more are included in this table except for two cities, Muskegon and Pontiac, where reports were not submitted.

Source: Unpublished reports of Michigan Community Chests to the Community Chests and Councils of America on Form CC-2, "1950 Receipts of Community Chest Agencies."

[4] Joint Legislative Committee to Study Foster Care, *Foster Care of Children in Michigan* (Lansing: Michigan State Department of Social Welfare, 1951), p. 244.

Table 3. Expenditures on Social Work Programs through State Governmental Departments in Michigan, 1950

Type of Program	Expenditures	Percent of Total
Public assistance	$100,974,217	95.0
Child welfare	2,721,551	2.5
School social work	486,075	.5
Services to the handicapped	1,224,328	1.0
Services to adult offenders	500,000 [a]	.5
Social work services in mental hospitals and clinics	500,000 [b]	.5
Total	$106,406,171	100.0

[a] This figure is an estimate and includes the total expenditures for individual treatment in the five state correctional institutions.
[b] This figure is an estimate. No state-wide figures separating social work services from other treatment services in the state mental hospitals and in the mental hygiene clinics receiving state funds are available.

Sources: Michigan Department of Social Welfare, *Annual Report Covering Fiscal Year 1949–50;* Michigan Department of Public Instruction, *Biennial Report 1948–49, 1949–50;* letter of November 27, 1951, from Michigan Department of Corrections.

social work expenditures and serve to indicate in general the amount of the expenditures and their distribution among social work programs.

Without further refining of the figures on expenditures it becomes clear that the people of Michigan have a substantial financial interest in the effective operation of the social work programs in the state. There is no readily available index by which the public can judge how well its money is being spent. In business the annual accounting which puts costs of operation in one column and returns from sales and services in the other provides a periodic and reliable indication of how well the business is being run. A business which shows an operating deficit for any length of time is automatically eliminated.

No such automatic control is operating to keep the obsolete or ineffective social work program from going on for some length of time on the basis of past momentum. Nor is there any readily understood and interpreted balance sheet which will single out the agency which is operating at a high level of efficiency.

Because social work, as so many other fields of governmental and voluntary activity, cannot rely on the profit and loss statement of business as a guide, it is all the more necessary to develop special means of keeping tabs on the effectiveness of agency operations. Every agency uses some type of "service accounting" which provides information about where the agency is investing its energies and resources. Few agencies make any attempt to carry on an accounting of results achieved. A few years ago, when the Board of Directors of the largest family casework agency in the country authorized a study "to determine and express how casework is carried on, at what cost, and with what success," it was news. Any agency today proposing such an undertaking in relation to its program is still going to make social work headlines.

THE PEOPLE SERVED

Totting up the financial investment of the community in social work programs is a dramatic way of pointing up the place of these programs in modern communities. More to the point, perhaps, is to note the number of people whose happiness and well-being is affected by these programs. Again, state-wide figures on the number of different individuals and families receiving social services in Michigan are not available, but figures are available for selected programs.

The public assistance programs serve the largest number of people. Following is the number of individuals as of January

1, 1950, who were receiving so-called categorical assistance, which comprises approximately 90 percent of the assistance granted in Michigan:

Category	Number of Recipients January 1, 1950
Old age assistance	98,743
Aid to dependent children	61,161
Aid to the blind	1,791

Approximately 8,600 children were receiving foster care through public and voluntary institutions and agencies as of January 1, 1950. Of these, 38 percent were in institutions and 62 percent in foster homes. Approximately 25,000 children were dealt with by the juvenile division of the probate courts during 1949, of whom three-fifths were brought before the court for delinquent behavior and two-fifths for other reasons, largely dependency or neglect.

No state-wide figures on persons served by voluntary agencies are compiled, but figures are available for Detroit. In Table 4 are figures on some selected programs in that city.[5]

The Detroit figures are admittedly unsatisfactory, based as they are on such different units as "cases" (which may include several persons in a family and involve one or several contacts in the course of a month), "patient visits," "annual memberships," etc. Undoubtedly the same persons are included in the figures for different programs. The figures give some notion, however, of the day-in, day-out flow of people to the voluntary social work agencies of the largest community in the state. If we could assume that workers in communities in the rest of the state provided about the same amount of service per worker as workers in Detroit, the Detroit figures could be slightly more than doubled to get a rough estimate of the persons in Michigan

[5] These figures are taken from *Social Statistics,* Statistical Bulletin of the Council of Social Agencies of Metropolitan Detroit, XI, No. 5 (1951), p. 3.

Table 4. Number of Cases or Persons Receiving Service from Selected Voluntary Social Work Programs, Detroit, 1950

Program	Number of Cases or Persons
Family service (monthly average of active cases)	3,298
Mental hygiene clinics (monthly average of patient visits)ʼ	2,829
Institutional care of the aged (daily average of individuals under care)	3,782
Institutional care of the transient and homeless (daily average of persons cared for)	1,560
Service to transients and travelers (monthly average of cases served)	2,839
Building-centered group work and recreation (total membership during year)	112,753
Non-building–centered group work and recreation (total membership during year)	90,373

receiving the services listed. This is possible because approximately 46 percent of the social workers in Michigan are in Detroit. Such an inflation of Detroit figures to obtain a state estimate is risky, however, because of important differences between the metropolitan area and the rest of the state.

THE INVESTMENT IN RESEARCH

When one tries to find out how much is being spent on research to evaluate and improve social work services, the information is scattered and incomplete. In Detroit, the Council of Social Agencies estimated it spent $24,000 on research in 1950; the Grand Rapids council estimated that it spent $2,500. No other councils or chests reported a specific appropriation for research work. The Michigan Department of Social Welfare operates an extensive statistical reporting system on the services it administers or supervises and conducts special studies from time to time on various phases of its program. No estimate is available on the cost of this activity because costs for statistics and financial accounting are difficult to separate. The Department of Corrections reports that it spent $21,600 in 1950 on research and statistics.

The schools of social work in the state all employ one faculty person with special responsibility for research, but this person's primary responsibility is for teaching and supervision of theses. In some instances other faculty members have undertaken to do research, the most noteworthy instance being Dr. Fritz Redl's work at Pioneer House and the Detroit Group Project. On the whole, the schools of social work have made no specific provision in their budgets for research, other than for teaching.

It would be an understatement to say that the investment of agencies and schools in research is out of line with their expenditures for current operations. Except for a kind of service accounting, research is almost nonexistent. Industry has learned that investment in research and development is the only way to assure survival in today's competitive markets. Medicine, where the goal is not increased profits but better ways of promoting health and combating disease, has long had a pattern of allocating substantial funds and personnel to research in hospitals and laboratories.

There are many reasons why social work has not included support of research as a regular part of its operating costs. One reason, perhaps, is its background in philanthropy. Scrutinizing results seems to run counter to the generous humanitarianism which traditionally has motivated the contributors to social work programs. A more fundamental reason has been the absence of the concepts and the tools by which research could solve the types of problems which social workers face in carrying on their day-by-day work. In spite of rapid strides in applied social research in the past fifteen years, this limitation still exists, but it is being pushed back every year. As Stuart Chase has said, "The argument that man is too unpredictable to be studied objectively is now . . . a dead issue. Only the ignorant raise it. A living body of genuine knowledge has been created. The war has advanced it in many departments. Already it can answer some of the problems of society better than any dictator, better than any convocation of elders, better than intuition or common sense." [6] Social work, along with all the other fields of practice in the art of human relations, stands to benefit by this developing body of knowledge.

In the preceding chapter we noted the mounting interest in research in social work on the part of laymen, practitioners, and scientists. This interest, if it is to be satisfied, will require a vastly different attitude than has prevailed in the past toward the allocation of funds for research in agencies, in councils of social agencies, and in schools of social work. In the concluding chapter of this report some specific recommendations on this point are presented.

Before talking about research budgets and an expanded research program, it is necessary to review the problems which confront social workers, the technical obstacles that stand in the way of getting answers to these problems, and the conditions for productive research in social work. To these topics the next three chapters are addressed.

[6] Stuart Chase, *The Proper Study of Mankind* (New York: Harper and Brothers, 1948), p. 46.

CHAPTER III

THE QUESTIONS WHICH CONCERN SOCIAL WORK

ONE OF THE FIRST steps in the Reconnaissance Study was to survey the kinds of questions which practitioners, administrators, and board members in social work were asking about the effectiveness of their programs. Such a survey has served two purposes. It has provided a roster of questions which can serve as a stimulus and guide to persons interested in undertaking evaluative research in social work. It has also brought out the way in which persons engaged in the day-by-day carrying-out of social work services see their problems.

As a means of getting a list of problems compiled, three conferences were held in Michigan during the spring of 1951. One conference was focused on problems in the field of child welfare, a second on problems in the family service field, and a third on problems in the field of public assistance. Other fields such as medical social work, probation and parole, and group work were not explored due to lack of time.

The conferences were attended by practitioners, agency administrators, community organization specialists, social work educators, representatives of related professions, and agency board members. Participants were asked to make their questions evaluative in character, although in the conferences many other types of questions were raised and some of these are included in this report. Participants were also told not to attempt to phrase or limit their questions in such a way as to make them researchable. The purpose of the conferences was not to outline a number of specific research projects, but to provide research workers in social work and in the social sciences a listing of problems which, from the standpoint of operating social work programs, need study. Some of the questions raised do not lend themselves to research at all, but fall in the field of values and ethics.

The discussion at the conferences was recorded on an electrical recorder and the questions transcribed and edited. The questions are presented in Appendix A. They are well worth careful study in terms of their content, but in this chapter we will confine ourselves to a consideration of what implications these questions have for a program of research in social work.

For purposes of discussion here and presentation in Appendix A, the questions have been grouped under six headings:

1) Questions about the goals of social work programs
2) Questions about the practical outcome of social work programs, practices, and policies
3) Questions about the assumptions and theories on which policy and practice rest
4) Questions about the influence of cultural, economic, and other social forces on the outcome of services
5) Questions about the effect of community attitudes and understanding on the effectiveness of social work services
6) Questions about the effect of social work practices and policies on attitudes and values in the community

The names of the persons who participated in the conferences are listed at the end of Appendix A.

QUESTIONS ABOUT THE GOALS OF SOCIAL WORK PROGRAMS

The first step in any kind of evaluative research is to come to some agreement on the goal that is being sought—what is considered success? It might be assumed that social work agencies dealing with similar problems would have the same objectives, but this is far from the case. In the field of services for unmarried mothers, for instance, one agency will regard separation of the child from the mother as desirable, an attitude deeply rooted in the philosophy of the agency. Another agency will proceed from an entirely different point of view, one which holds as primary the right of the child to stay with his mother. The difference between these agencies in treatment objectives reflects more basic differences in the ethical and value systems underlying the programs of the agencies. To conduct meaningful evaluative research on the services of either agency would mean first specifying what each agency was trying to achieve.

A good many of the questions raised in the conferences were questions about goals, and like all value judgments they depend in the final analysis on the exercise of choice. What contribution, then, can research make in relation to the question of the goals of social work programs? The questions raised by the conferees indicated at least three ways in which research might contribute.

First, research can determine what the goals are which are held by different groups concerned with social services—the client, the practitioner, the board member, the financial contributor. Secondly, it can determine, in at least some situations, whether specific operating goals are contributing to realization of more general goals. Thus in a juvenile correctional institution an immediate goal might be to make a child conform to the rules and routines of the institution. This immediate goal might or might not lead to realization of the general goal of returning the child to society in such a condition that he will not continue to violate society's rules. A third contribution of research in relation to goals is to suggest alternative measures for achieving goals which may not occur to those carrying responsibility for operating existing programs. In the field of dentistry the fluoridation of water to retard tooth decay is a measure which might not occur to practitioners absorbed in filling teeth and making dentures. In social work an economist or anthropologist may see approaches to problems which the practitioner is not apt to consider.

Perhaps the most striking outcome of the discussion about goals of social work programs in the conferences was the need for agencies to be much more specific about what they are seeking to achieve. Particularly in those agencies whose original purposes have been modified to meet changing conditions in society is this important. Only as goals are made quite explicit is it possible to consciously direct agency operations toward efficient goal attainment. Research can assist materially in identifying and clarifying goals. Ultimately, of course, determination of goals must rest upon certain value assumptions which are beyond scientific validation. Research is frequently indispensable, however, in establishing the links between the value assumptions and the specific goals of operations.

QUESTIONS ABOUT THE PRACTICAL OUTCOME OF SOCIAL
WORK PROGRAMS, PRACTICES, AND POLICIES

By far the largest number of questions raised in the conferences centered around the practical outcome of specific practices and policies in social work programs. These questions were of the "proof of the pudding is in the eating" type. It is the kind of proof in which everyone is interested. A glance through these questions in Appendix A will suggest how difficult it is apt to be to get prompt and definitive answers. The Reconnaissance Study has proceeded on the assumption, however, that for an operating field which is daily confronted with the necessity of choice and of action, research which does not eventuate in answers as to the practical outcome of policies and practices will not receive acceptance and support.

It will be helpful to consider the questions in this group under several subheadings.

Questions about the merits of alternative policies or programs.—Social work is full of "natural experiments," that is, situations where the same operation is being carried out under different policies or with different techniques. In some instances there are fairly simple alternatives, the outcome of which can be quite readily compared. In some instances the alternatives being considered are made up of a number of elements, and it may be very difficult to identify the significant elements which are being compared.

Thus it is relatively simple to compare the outcome of adoptive placements, made by the same agency, where the child is under six months of age with the outcome of placements where the child is two years of age. A much more complex problem is posed when an attempt is made to compare adoptions arranged through agencies with adoptions arranged through private individuals. A study conceivably could show no significant difference between agency and private adoptions and be quite misleading if no account had been taken of differences of skill existing among adoption agencies. Or the lack of difference might be due to the type of child who is placed with an agency for adoption as contrasted with the type of child whom private individuals may undertake to place. Factors which might invalidate comparisons in a study of this kind are not so obscure, however, that the more significant ones could not be taken into account.

In both the "natural experiments" in the adoption field mentioned there are, of course, numerous technical research problems such as devising a reliable method of rating the success of adoptive placements, but again, this kind of obstacle should not prove insurmountable.

It is when we get to such questions as the following one, posed by a worker in a psychiatrically oriented children's agency, that we encounter alternatives which are made up of so many elements that reliable comparisons would be exceedingly difficult to make: "What is the effectiveness of adoption agency programs where placement is based on a physical and psychometric study of the child as compared with agencies where in addition to these studies there is a study of the inner emotional life of the child?"

This type of question is the kind which leads us to ask whether there may not be more economical and precise ways of comparing one practice or policy with another than field studies of existing programs. There are. The point here is that this question as phrased by a practitioner needs considerable reformulation to make it amenable to research or, perhaps more accurately, to make it amenable to the kind of research which would not cost far more than most organizations are able or willing to spend for an answer.

Questions about the outcome of a particular welfare program or policy, with no alternative program or policy specified.—It is one thing to determine through research which of two or more specified alternatives comes nearest to producing the results sought. It is something else to pose for research the general question of the "results" of a particular program or policy.

At one extreme we get the general type of question raised, such as: what happens to the attitudes and personalities of people who have been on relief for a long time? To make this question meaningful there would have to be specified, among other things: (a) the types of attitudes and the personality characteristics to be examined; (b) the policies under which the relief was administered; (c) the skill of the personnel administering the relief; (d) the cultural setting in which the relief was administered (were 5 percent or 50 percent of the neighbors also receiving relief?); (e) the adequacy of the relief, etc. There may be ten or twenty other things that should also be specified. This is the kind of question which is all-important but unanswerable, through research, in the form in which it is stated. Making this a question susceptible of research, or rather outlining the subquestions which together add up to the main question, is a job which calls for a thorough grasp of the possibilities and limitations of research technique and the practical and theoretical knowledge which may bear on the answer.

To recognize this kind of question as difficult or as made up of a great many subquestions, however, is not to suggest that it be avoided. The question will obviously need a careful reformulation, and there must be vigilance lest in reformulation the original question is lost.

At the other extreme we find specific, limited questions which can be answered in exactly the terms in which the question is asked. Take, for instance, the question, "What happens to applicants for public assistance who are rejected because of lack of residence—do they accept referral back to their place of residence, how many stay on in their new community and work out something else, and how satisfactory is this new arrangement?" A fairly accurate answer to a question of this kind can be produced. In this case, however, a problem is posed by the specific and limited nature of the question. Residence requirements are part of a larger pattern of locally financed relief expenditures, and research on the effect of residence requirements might produce more usable answers if it were related to the larger problem, namely, "How finance and administer public assistance in a time of high mobility of labor, a mobility essential to a flexible and changing economy?"

This larger context might suggest classifying the nonresident applicants into those engaged in seasonal labor, those engaged in industries working the year round, those brought into an area in connection with defense contracts, those who because of age or physical incapacity are not potential members of the labor force, etc. An answer which took into account these and perhaps other significant groupings among the nonresident population would have much more practical usefulness to the public welfare agency dealing with this problem.

Our brief review of the above two questions indicates that questions can be both too general and too specific. Asking the right question in the right form, as Stuart Chase has observed, is half the battle in research, and in a field of practice like social work it calls for participation by both the researcher and the practitioner or policy maker. Any plan for a continuing program of research in social work will have to provide for this kind of participation in the question-asking phase of the research.

Questions about the results of social work policies or programs as compared with their costs.—Most questions about results in social work programs are related in one way or another to costs. Cost accounting has become an integral part of any industrial activity and provides the basis for many improvements. So far, cost accounting in social work is at only a very elementary stage. One of the reasons is that it is so difficult to judge what any particular result is worth in financial terms. How much is it worth to achieve matching of adoptive parents and adoptive child in 85 percent instead of 55 percent of the cases? What is it worth to make the receipt of financial assistance in old age a less humiliating experience than it otherwise might be?

Some of the questions focused on costs which are measurable during the period that services are being given: Are interviews which cost $15.00 under a plan of detailed recording and supervision as effective as interviews which cost $7.50 under a plan of minimum recording and supervision? What is the comparative cost of foster care and homemaker service in relatively short-term´ cases? What is the cost of a program of financial assistance which provides bare subsistence as compared with a program which involves heavy initial expenditures for rehabilitation but results in the client's becoming self-supporting after a year or so?

Some questions focus on long-range costs which must be borne by society; these costs the particular agency providing service does not have to consider. Typical of such questions is the one frequently asked about the cost of supporting an adult criminal in prison as compared with the cost of preventive services to head off delinquent careers.

With budget and appropriating bodies as cost conscious as they are, it is curious that there has been so little definitive research on such questions as have just been raised. Margaret Blenkner has summarized in an excellent fashion the obstacles which have stood in the way of evaluative research in casework, and the summary applies to other areas of social work as well.[1] If space permitted, her analysis might well be incorporated as part of this report. She classifies the obstacles as psychological, economic, social, and methodological. And not the least among the obstacles is the costliness of sound research. This obstacle is apt to remain a stumbling block until there are a few convincing demonstrations of the infinitely greater cost of leaving research undone.

[1] Margaret Blenkner, "Obstacles to Evaluative Research in Casework," *Social Casework*, February and March, 1950, pp. 54–60 and 97–105.

Questions about the effect of qualifications of personnel on the quality of service provided.—In the development of social work as a professional field, the central focus has been on improving the qualifications of personnel providing social work services. This is precisely what might be expected in a profession which puts so much stress on the *way* in which help is given, not simply on the help itself. This emphasis on personnel qualifications has resulted in the development of policies and practices for the recruitment, training, employment, and promotion of staff in social agencies. A good many questions were raised in the conferences, therefore, not only on the relation between qualifications of personnel and quality of service, but also on the effectiveness of various recruitment, training, and employment policies and practices in producing qualified personnel.

An example of the questions concerning the relationship of personnel and quality of service is one asked by a child welfare worker. She wanted information on the comparative effectiveness of a foster home placement agency staffed with trained social workers and an agency staffed with untrained workers. It is the kind of question which, if a simple answer could be given, would have tremendous budgetary and other implications. It does not take much reflection, however, to see how complex this kind of question really is. Could two agencies be found where the tangible services provided were identical, except that in one case they were administered through trained, and in the other case through untrained workers? And what is meant by "trained"? Would the "trained" workers all be considered similar, even though some had been trained in the so-called "functional" school of social casework, while others had been trained in the so-called "diagnostic" school; or some had two years of training and no experience, and others had one year of training and six years of experience? Such questions come immediately to mind, and a researcher tackling the problem would find many more such questions.

This is one of those central problems in social work where the proof-of-the-pudding-is-in-the-eating approach is not apt to provide the quickest or the most definitive answer. Devising sound and economical approaches to questions of this kind is one of the central tasks of a research program in social work and one which calls for the fullest possible use of the knowledge and experience in related fields as well as in social work. The Institute for Human Adjustment at the University of Michigan recently completed a study in which it sought to identify the characteristics that make for successful practice in the field of clinical psychology. Such a study may have a bearing on selection of persons for some positions in social work, but to make appropriate use of this study and others like it calls for thorough understanding of the research procedures used so as to avoid their misapplication to social work.

Numerous specific questions were raised as to the effectiveness of one or another device for producing qualified personnel. In connection with these questions it should be noted that a three-year study has just been completed which looked at only one of the devices for obtaining qualified social workers, namely education.[2] It found numerous shortcomings in social work education as presently organized and carried out. It was limited in its findings and recommendations, however, by the absence of a thoroughgoing analysis of the content of the social work job, or more accurately, jobs. How can curriculum and teaching methods to prepare persons for the variety of responsibilities in social work be planned until there is a clear analysis of the skills and the knowledge which are called for in doing

[2] Ernest V. Hollis and Alice L. Taylor, *Social Work Education in the United States* (New York: Columbia University Press, 1951).

social work? The authors say, "The profession has only begun to make systematic studies of the actual tasks performed by social workers in the principal types of jobs to show the content, complexity, and degrees of responsibility of each major duty." [3] The bearing of this observation by Dr. Hollis and Miss Taylor on our discussion here is to underscore the existence of preliminary tasks which must be faced in most evaluative research undertakings. We are back again to the point already made that the task of phrasing questions and organizing them into a logical sequence is an exceedingly difficult one and is truly half the research battle. The fact that this task has been done up to now in such a spotty and incomplete way poses one of the problems for which any continuing research program in social work must make provision.

Questions about the adequacy of various administrative policies or structures for achieving the goals of social work programs.—The questions about administrative policies and organization properly come under the previous questions about the outcome of various policies and practices, but they deal with a sufficiently different kind of problem that they are presented separately.

Administration is, strictly speaking, a means to an end, a facilitating kind of activity which finds its only justification in the end product of the agency—service to clients. Looked at this way, administration starts off with an acceptance of the service as valid and is concerned with how it can be provided most efficiently. Some persons may protest this narrow a construction of administration, pointing to its role in formulating objectives. This protest is proper, but since we have treated the question of goals and objectives under a separate section, we will direct attention here to administration as a device for implementing goals.

[3] *Ibid.*, p. 12.

As might be anticipated, questions about administration are of the how-to-do-it type, and in this sense they fall almost wholly in the area of engineering research. Take the question, "What is the optimum size caseload for a worker in a family service agency?" This is the kind of question in which there are so many contingent factors that a specific answer would probably be valid only for the particular agency or type of agency studied. Involved in the answer to this question would be the type of problem coming to the agency, the skill of the workers, the "treatment goal" of the agency, the kind of treatment procedures followed, etc. Once these variables, or combinations of them, were specified, it should be possible to arrive at an answer as to the optimum size caseload. The conditional clause, "once these variables were specified," however, takes in a great deal of territory. In this case it implies, among other things, having a way of classifying problems in terms of their difficulty and their susceptibility to treatment, a method of rating workers' skill, a clearly specified treatment goal, and a means of determining the extent to which it has been realized. But these preliminary tools for research on this problem do not exist today, or they exist only in crude form.

The question of optimum size caseload brings out a problem that must be faced in all engineering research, namely, what degree of precision and reliability must be attached to the answer? And would the research required to produce an answer of a given degree of precision be feasible or economically justifiable? In the case of optimum size caseloads for family service agencies, most of which employ less than five workers, perhaps the research investment for a precise and highly reliable answer would not be justified. What may be called for here is a refinement of the judgment which administrators and supervisors bring to this problem, a refinement in which the use of logic, common sense, experience, and a certain amount of fact-finding would be dominant. Refinement of judgment can proceed much further, however, as the products and by-products of research become available. As research begins to produce classifications of the problems and personalities of clients, as it devises methods for measuring the results of treatment, the administrator will have a sounder basis for his judgment.

QUESTIONS ABOUT THE ASSUMPTIONS AND THEORIES ON
WHICH POLICY AND PRACTICE REST

Every policy or practice in social work rests on some assumption or theory which may or may not be explicit. Thus the assumption behind the Elizabethan Poor Law was that people are in want because of their own shiftlessness and laziness and the way to motivate them to become self-supporting is to label them publicly and to grant them the barest subsistence rations. Some theories are of this homespun type, some are based on ethical or religious beliefs, some are explanations by professional social workers which seek to account for facts encountered in day-by-day experience, and some are theories which have come out of research in the sciences and in related professions.

One of the economies in identifying theories underlying practices or policies is that once this is done it becomes possible to examine the theories in light of a much larger body of knowledge and, perhaps, to avoid the expensive and arduous task of examining the outcome of a practice or policy in particular situations. Thus instead of an expensive follow-up over a long period of years to determine the effect on adoptive children of keeping them in an institution until they are two years old, it should be possible to apply what is known about child development during the first two years of life and then determine whether the crucial needs for this development are or are not met in an institutional setting. The whole genius of human learning, brought to its highest development in modern science, is this procedure of generalizing about life's experiences and then applying the generalizations to new situations without having to carry on a costly trial-and-error approach every time a new problem is encountered.

There were comparatively few questions raised about assumptions or theories underlying social work practice because the conferences were focused on results of practice. Inevitably, however, assumptions and theories were discussed. To the questions raised in the conferences and included in Appendix A has been added a list which was compiled by a faculty committee of the New York School of Social Work. The questions suggest something of the scope of the task of simply making explicit the assumptions and theories underlying social work programs and practices.

QUESTIONS ABOUT THE INFLUENCE OF CULTURAL,
ECONOMIC, AND OTHER SOCIAL FORCES ON
THE OUTCOME OF SERVICES

Evaluative questions inevitably lead to questions about the influence of environmental factors. In the early days of World War II social workers saw persons whom they had not been able to help through individualized casework services suddenly become self-directing, self-supporting individuals. The reason was simple. They were wanted in the economy. All kinds of marginal individuals were able to get along who had not been able to before—the aged, the physically handicapped, the mentally retarded, the young and inexperienced. No social work program can be evaluated in a vacuum; it must be seen in relation to the kind of forces against which it is contending.

Because of social work's special responsibility to step into situations where the regular institutions in the community have failed to operate satisfactorily for particular individuals or groups, it has to have as wide as possible an understanding of the social forces that are at work. Among the forces about which participants raised questions were racial discrimination in relation to employment, economic deprivation in relation to delinquent behavior, and the impact of a war-boom community on the stability of family life.

QUESTIONS ABOUT THE EFFECT OF COMMUNITY ATTITUDES
AND UNDERSTANDING ON THE EFFECTIVENESS OF SOCIAL
WORK SERVICES

The effectiveness of a social work service depends not only on how well it is performed, but also on how well the community understands the service and is willing to make use of it. A number of questions came up on the influence of community attitudes on the effectiveness of social work programs. Some community attitudes are so deeply rooted in our culture that they must be accepted and adjusted to, at least in terms of an agency's immediate job. The receipt of public assistance as meaning "going on the county" is so deeply rooted in the minds of some older people that even the most progressive policies and skilled program of interpretation are not going to change their attitudes toward applying for assistance. On the other hand, some attitudes are susceptible to change and might be modified by a proper program of interpretation and community education.

One participant reported that a family service agency in a populous community had been closed recently because it had only six clients, while in this same community a trade union was starting a counseling service to help its members. She asked why the family agency had not been able to attract union members to it.

Whether the attitudes among union members toward use of the family service agency, or perhaps their complete ignorance of it, could be modified by the agency is an open question. Bertha Reynolds has suggested that the sense of "belonging" which a trade union member brings to a counseling service in his own union is a crucial factor in his ability to use the service. Here, at any rate, is a matter for research where the problem lies in the attitudes of people before they ever come in contact with the agency, and the research on the problem would have to go on outside the walls of the agency to a considerable extent.

Agencies carry on various activities to change attitudes in the community toward use of their service. Several instances were mentioned where the understanding and skill of the individual worker are as important as the work of a centralized public relations program in modifying attitudes in the community. In parole work, success depends to a large extent on parole workers being able to modify attitudes of individual employers toward former criminals. In rehabilitation of the blind a problem of like nature is encountered. In adoption agencies the worker's skill in dealing with disappointed applicants for adoptive children is a crucial factor in combating the black market in babies and getting support for sound adoption practices.

The questions raised reveal how central is the problem of community understanding of agency services in the successful provision of these services. They also suggest the potential contribution of research to improve agencies' efforts in this area by bringing out the nature and the sources of attitudes in the community toward their programs.

QUESTIONS ABOUT THE EFFECT OF SOCIAL WORK PRACTICES
AND POLICIES ON ATTITUDES AND VALUES IN THE
COMMUNITY

The need to evaluate the effect of social work policies and programs, not only on the individuals receiving help but also on attitudes and values in the larger community, came out in the conferences. The largest social work program, public assistance, is perhaps the most dramatic example of a social work program which itself has become a factor which molds attitudes in the community, as well as reflects them.

Participants raised questions about the effect of a pension-type program on the sense of responsibility of children for their parents and on the vitality of the family as an institution; about the effect of the social security program on the attitude of people toward work and their responsibility for providing for their own future; and about the effect of the sixty-five year age limit in the social security program on the interest of older people in continuing in productive employment.

Questions of this type came frequently from the conference participants who were not engaged professionally in social work. Their questions suggest the value in any research program of making provision for the representation of the community-centered, as contrasted with profession-centered, point of view. This point of view should be expected among board members of social agencies and also among sociologists and economists who are concerned professionally with the functioning of the larger community.

SUMMARY

There are several implications for planning a program of research in social work which come out of this review of the questions raised in the conferences of the spring of 1951.

First, it is important to note that certain questions facing social work are questions about goals and values—what are the end results that are being sought? These questions cannot be answered, in the final analysis, by research but depend on the making of choices and decisions by those responsible for social work programs. Research can contribute to these choices and decisions, however, by providing factual information on which they can be based and by making explicit the reasoning and the evidence which underlie the assumption that immediate goals are contributing to the ultimate goals of the social work program.

Secondly, the review of the questions has brought out how crucial is the task of phrasing questions and organizing them into an appropriate sequence for research. Problems are so complex as they arise in operating programs that it becomes necessary to break them down into a series of subquestions of manageable size. The process of question reformulation calls for knowledge of the possibilities and limitations of research and of the concepts that may have a bearing on the questions. At the same time it is important to guard against losing the original question in the process of reformulating it, and this means that both the research specialist and the practitioner and policy maker must be involved in the process of question formulation.

Isidor Chein has commented cogently on the hazards connected with the formulation and selection of questions for research. His comments merit a slight diversion from our summary.[4] He urges, first, that research in an applied field deal with problems about which it is possible to do something. Otherwise the research is apt to result in a contribution to science but to have little use in advancing the operations or ultimate objectives of agencies. He urges, secondly, that the practitioner stand guard over the reformulation of questions lest in reducing the problem to a research design the life shall have gone out of it. And he urges, finally, that steps be taken to insure that those responsible for applying findings have sufficient understanding and faith in them to apply them. There

---

[4] Isidor Chein, "Some Aspects of Research Methodology," *The Jewish Social Service Quarterly*, XXV, No. 4 (June, 1949), pp. 452–57.

has recently been completed in a large university a piece of research on the validity of certain psychological tests used by social agencies. The research is sound, but the people who are supposed to be guided by the findings do not understand and have no confidence in the research procedures followed. The result is that the outcome of the research is being discounted before it is even published. Somehow the questions of the practitioner about research procedures must be dealt with if the findings are going to be applied.

Returning to our summary, we should note thirdly that the review of questions has brought out the number of preliminary tasks which must be undertaken to make possible evaluative research in social work. The answers to the problems in an applied field are apt to be the end product of a long line of research. The quick way to answers of this type does not lie in starting immediately to build the end product, but in devising the necessary concepts and tools which will make the end product possible.

Fourthly, the importance of making explicit the assumptions and theories underlying social work has come out. Once these are stated they can be considered in the context of a much larger body of knowledge. Indeed, the research may consist largely of "translating" established theory in the sciences and in other professions into terms that apply to the social work operation under study.

In the next chapter we turn to a systematic examination of the steps involved in doing evaluative research and consider the success with which some representative studies have carried out these steps.

CHAPTER IV

THE LOGIC OF
EVALUATIVE RESEARCH

THERE ARE certain steps which are essential to any kind of evaluative thinking. They are much the same whether the subject under consideration is a new weapon, a new strain of hybrid corn, or a social work program. Together these steps make up what is called here "the logic of evaluative research," and any evaluative undertaking has to deal with them in one way or another.

In this chapter we will review first what these steps are. We will turn then to an examination of the way in which the steps have been carried out in some selected studies in social work.

THE STEPS IN EVALUATIVE RESEARCH

The essential steps in evaluative thinking have already emerged in our discussion of questions which concern social work in the preceding chapter. They may be summarized under five headings: (1) identifying the goals that are being sought; (2) analyzing the problems with which the activity—in our case, social work—must cope; (3) describing and standardizing this activity; (4) measuring the degree of change that comes about; and (5) determining whether the change observed is the result of the activity or due to some other cause.

In order to consider these five steps in relation to a fairly simple problem—simple as compared with evaluating social work programs, at least—let us look at the steps which any industrious homeowner is apt to go through in deciding how best to get a velvety smooth turf established around his new suburban home.

Identifying the goals sought.—Lawns serve different purposes. Our homeowner will have to decide whether he wants a decorative green carpet as a setting for his house or a rugged turf that can stand up under back-yard football. He may refine his goals by looking for a lawn that will stand up under August drought while he is off on vacation or one that will take weed-killing chemicals without shriveling up. Until he knows what he is after he will not be able to decide between the alleged merits of Kentucky bluegrass or Chewings fescue, clover or bent grass.

The goals of social work programs are usually not as simple or as readily identifiable as the goals of our lawn builder, as the questions reviewed in the last chapter have indicated. Furthermore, the goals of the professional worker may differ from those of the community chest contributor and the goals of the user of the social service may differ from both of these. Agreement on goals and criteria of success is essential, however, if evaluation is going to have meaning for the various groups concerned.

Analyzing the problem.—Looking over his muddy plot, our homeowner is going to try to assess what he is up against in establishing a successful lawn. He may have slopes or areas of shade to contend with, or a low spot that needs draining, or clay soil that needs some humus dug into it. Knowing just what his problem is calls for a good deal of technical knowledge. And if he overlooks one of the important factors, all his work on the lawn may go for nought. He may follow the prescription of his neighbor who has a perfect lawn and end up with a scraggly turf that dies in late summer because the soil is acid.

Analyzing the problem is the same thing as knowing what are the variables that influence the growth of a lawn. And while there are enough variables in lawn building to account for a substantial body of literature, they are simple as compared with the variables the researcher encounters when he tries to determine what factors have brought about the need for social work services and may influence the effectiveness of those services.

Describing and standardizing the activity.—Having formed some diagnosis of his problem, our homeowner will proceed next to prepare his soil, plant his seed, and then tend the new grass while it is growing. What he does will be guided by the end result he has set for himself and the particular assortment of problems with which he sees himself confronted. He may dig in some peat moss, sow a mixture of quick-growing cover grasses and slow-growing permanent grasses, scatter some commercial fertilizer, water conscientiously during the period of seed germination, etc.

With all this, his lawn may still turn out a miserable failure, depending on how he carries out his various operations. He may cover his seed so deeply it comes up sparsely and late, he may burn the seed by improper application of the fertilizer, he may compact his ground by using too heavy a roller, or he may do all these things correctly but pick out the wrong time of the year in which to do them. When he takes his problem to the proprietor of the seed store or to the county agricultural agent he will be asked about his lawn-growing procedures and unless he can report them accurately he will not be able to find out what went wrong.

In social work the problem of making sure not only that the proper services are provided to meet the particular need of a client or group of clients, but also that they are provided in accordance with specified methods is infinitely more complex than the problem our homeowner faced. Indeed, it is not just the things the social worker or the agency does that are important, but also the things other persons may be doing over which the social worker has little control. How to control these other factors, or at least take them into account in determining what has happened and why, is one of the factors that limits the precision of any social research, as contrasted with the test tube kind of research which has made possible the tremendous advances in the physical sciences.

Measuring the degree of change.—Most lawn builders are not going to be too fussy about a precise measure of how well their lawn turns out. But if our homeowner is trying to compare a procedure used in one part of the yard with the procedure used in another, he will have to devise some measure for comparing them.

The first thing he will have to decide is when he is going to judge his lawn. Will he judge it at the end of the first growing season, or at the end of the second growing season? If he judges it too soon, he will be misled by the luxuriant annual grasses that will die out in one year. If he waits too long, so many other things will have occurred to affect the lawn that he cannot be sure that any failures are properly attributable to the lawn-building procedures he followed. It is even more difficult in social work than in lawn building to decide just when the results of activities should be evaluated.

The mechanics of a measuring device for rating the degree of success he has achieved will pose problems to our homeowner. The same problem in infinitely more complex form confronts social work. The source material is difficult to get at and not too reliable. The researcher may simply have to accept the workers' account of the client's adjustment—not a very objective source. Devising a scale for rating the various degrees of improvement that may have occurred is difficult, and applying the scale to individual cases is both time-consuming and costly. But the task of measurement cannot be avoided.

Determining cause-effect relationships.—If our homeowner is not to be badly led astray as to the things that made him succeed or fail in his project, he will have to work out some way of determining cause-effect relationships. He may have bought an expensive new hormone-treated seed and attribute all his success to this, unless by chance he used up some ordinary seed he had around the place and found it did just as well. Or he may blame the late application of a fertilizer for the fact that his lawn turned brown in August, when his real problem was that he watered so superficially that the grass roots were all at the surface and were killed by the summer sun.

There is only one method he can use for pinning down cause-effect relationships, and this is to compare two parts of his lawn where as many relevant factors as possible were kept identical except one, such as the type of seed which he planted. If the part with his fancy seed turns out better, he has pretty good evidence for continuing to buy this seed. If both parts of the lawn are equally bad, he will not know much about the comparative merits of ordinary and hormone-treated seeds, but he will know that something besides type of seed caused his failure.

All scientific research goes back to one form or another of this type of comparison. Astronomers cannot rearrange the stars to test their theories; they have to work out elaborate observational techniques for getting the comparisons they need. Social scientists may have to study an aboriginal tribe in Australia and the Hollywood movie colony to get the comparisons they need. Methods of getting at cause-effect relationships in the field of human growth and human relations are available, however, and have been improved vastly in the last twenty years as a result of new developments in statistical technique. These methods can be applied in determining the effectiveness of social work programs. The answers produced will not be as precise as the answers chemists can get from their experiments. And it may seem that the methods are more successful in debunking old theories than in introducing new ones that work. But so far no one has found a way of escaping the final step, in the logic of evaluative research, of establishing causal relationships by some type of experimental design.

A REVIEW OF SOME EVALUATIVE STUDIES IN SOCIAL WORK

There are a limited number of studies in social work to which we can turn in reviewing the problems and the achievements of evaluative research in this field. Three such studies have been analyzed in detail for this report and a fourth study, which is concerned with prediction rather than evaluation, has also been examined.

The discussion of these studies is not intended to provide a balanced and comprehensive review of the problems and possibilities of evaluative research in social work. To have done this would have required a much larger group of studies, selected so as to represent various types of evaluative undertakings. The four studies reviewed here serve to bring out enough of the problems and to suggest enough of the possibilities for purposes of a reconnaissance operation. They also provide us some solid illustrative material to which to tie our thinking when we consider the requirements for evaluative research in social work.

It will be worth while for the reader before getting much further into this chapter to turn to Appendix B and read the analyses of the four studies. These analyses were prepared by consultants to the Reconnaissance Study who had either worked on the projects or had special knowledge of the kind of research under consideration. One study, analyzed by Leon Festinger, is concerned with community services in a housing project; another study, analyzed by John Hill, is concerned with family casework services; a third study, analyzed by Helen Witmer, is concerned with a program of prevention of juvenile delinquency; and a fourth study, analyzed by Alfred Kahn, is concerned with prediction of juvenile delinquency.[1] Each consultant was given an outline of the way in which he was to cover the steps in evaluative research so that the analyses would be comparable. The analysis by Alfred Kahn, being concerned with prediction instead of evaluation, does not adhere to the outline.

A reading of the analyses will reveal the success with which the five steps in evaluative research were carried out in the projects under consideration. Here we will center our attention on the implications of the successes and shortcomings for planning a program for evaluative research in social work.

It should be noted that in the discussion which follows we are not concerned with the type of agency evaluations which are conducted to determine whether an agency measures up to certain standards which have been adopted for its particular type of program. The Child Welfare League of America, for instance, conducts such evaluations. In studying an agency it does not attempt to find out how the children dealt with by

[1] The exact names of these studies and their authors follow:

Changing Attitudes through Social Contact, by Leon Festinger and Harold Kelly (Ann Arbor: Research Center for Group Dynamics, Institute for Social Research, University of Michigan, 1951).

Measuring Results in Social Casework: A Manual on Judging Movement, by J. McVicker Hunt and Leonard S. Kogan (New York: Family Service Association of America, 1950).

An Experiment in the Prevention of Delinquency, by Edwin Powers and Helen Witmer (New York: Columbia University Press, 1951).

Unraveling Juvenile Delinquency, by Sheldon and Eleanor Glueck (New York: The Commonwealth Fund, 1950).

the agency actually turn out, but seeks to determine whether the agency conforms to certain standards of child welfare practice which the League has adopted. If the League finds that the agency employs trained workers, has a low rate of staff turnover, pays adequate boarding rates, has provision for diagnostic study of the child before placement, assigns reasonable size caseloads, etc., the conclusion is that it is doing an effective job. Such evaluative studies are essential for administrative or planning purposes but they are not the kind of studies we are considering here.

Identifying the goals sought.—As we have noted, in order to evaluate any kind of activity we have to know what it is we are trying to achieve. The goals in social work programs may be put into a hierarchy at the top of which are broad, philosophic objectives, and at the bottom of which is a whole series of specific, limited goals which lead toward, or are assumed to lead toward, realization of the broad objectives.

Research in relation to broad objectives is not possible until the objectives are put into "operational" terms. To take the goal of character-building as an example, the particular kinds of behavior and attitudes which are included in the concept "good character" have to be specified before research on the extent of their realization can go forward.

Operational goals can always be found to underlie policy and practice in social agencies, but typically the first task of the research investigator is to make them explicit. This task may itself require some research. In one of the studies reviewed in Appendix B, the study of movement in social casework conducted by Hunt and his associates, a bit of research was done to get at operational goals. Hunt had practitioners rate cases as improved or unimproved and then asked them what factors in the cases caused them to come to their conclusions. The factors they pointed to he found could be classified under a number of headings, which were finally reduced to four: removal of disabling habits and conditions, increase in adaptive efficiency, improved verbalized attitudes and understanding, and improved environmental conditions. These then became the operational goals against which movement of cases was judged.

Objections to the goals of casework identified by Hunt have been raised, notably by Philip Klein. Klein's position is that these were the goals which practitioners in one agency were seeking in relation to a relatively small portion of their clients and do not necessarily represent the goals of casework in the wide variety of settings where it is practiced. In his own words, "the essential social value of casework becomes identified [in Hunt's study] with the specific objectives of one type of agency, operating under a particular intake policy, relating to a small faction of its own case load, conditioned by particular psychoanalytic and procedural commitments, and oriented to technical ends rather than to social needs. . . ." [2] Klein's criticism is really not directed at the movement scale as such, but at the possible misapplications of it which he fears. If the scale were entitled "criteria for judging movement as seen by caseworkers in long-term treatment cases receiving service in the Community Service Society of New York City during the 1940's" Klein's criticisms of the movement scale would be largely met, except that he might still question the investment of scarce research resources in research which was as "proprietary" or agency-centered as the movement scale necessarily is.

The real significance of the movement scale would be missed if the instrument itself were regarded as the major product of the research. The major product of the three years Hunt and

[2] Philip Klein, "Past and Future in Social Welfare Research," *The Social Welfare Forum, 1951.* Official Proceedings, 78th Annual Meeting of the National Conference of Social Work (New York: Columbia University Press, 1951), p. 138.

his associates worked on this scale was the development of a procedure for creating movement scales, a procedure which now can be followed in developing scales applicable to child-placing agencies, juvenile courts, medical social work programs, and other programs where the problems presented and the goals sought are different from those at the Community Service Society.

It is important to note that Hunt did not go beyond the caseworkers in trying to find out what were the goals of case-work practice in the Community Service Society. For purposes of his research, he assumed their goals and the agency's goals were identical. A further study might well be conducted to ascertain the extent to which there is agreement among board members, administrators, and caseworkers as to the goals of the agency. Another study might seek to find out how clients and persons referring clients understand the goals of the agency.

This kind of exploration might well precede the development of detailed measuring instruments. If it is discovered that there is not agreement among board and staff and community on the problems which the agency accepts and the goals it sets in dealing with these problems, it might be well to post-pone the research. Research findings about the extent to which practitioners are attaining their goals will not be of much significance to others who question the propriety of their goals. On the other hand, where the research is not for administrative or planning purposes in a particular agency, but is focused on the relative effectiveness of alternative procedures followed by casework practitioners, it is enough if immediate goals are specified and their relationship, or assumed relationship, to broader social goals clarified.

It is characteristic of scientific research to break problems down into small units in order to conduct studies with any degree of precision. There is an understandable tendency on the part of practitioners and policy makers to be impatient with the circumscribed area which the researcher marks out for study. However, science has progressed as innumerable small researches, carried on within a common framework of scientific method and theory, have gradually built up a composite picture which has practical significance for policy and practice. All that can be asked of research in social work is that attention be given in launching research to making explicit the relationship of the particular project to the problems demanding solution by those operating social work programs.

Analyzing the problem.—In our review of the task confronting the homeowner trying to get a lawn established we said that analyzing his problem was the same as deciding what the factors are that influence the growth of the kind of lawn he wanted. It is in this sense that we are discussing the analysis of the problem or problems confronting a social work program.

There is always a fairly clearly recognized "presenting problem" with which agencies start. In public assistance it is the lack of money to maintain a minimum standard of living as defined by the community. In foster care for children it is the inability of parents to rear their own children. This presenting problem is the agency's reason for being. Indeed, it is the starting point from which the goals of the agency have been defined.

However, the presenting problem is frequently the result of one or more quite distinct causative or contributing problems. Social agency programs are concerned with understanding these causative or contributing problems as well as seeking to alleviate the presenting problem. As the agency's understanding of the causative or contributing problems increases, the agency is able to plan more intelligently its efforts to deal with the presenting problem. Caste barriers in a community, for instance, may be at the root of problems with which an agency is trying to cope in an interracial youth center or club program. The fact that the agency cannot change these barriers does not mean that an understanding of their operation is unimportant. Understanding will point the way toward measures which are feasible for the agency, thus avoiding misplaced effort, and also will suggest approaches which fall outside the responsibility of the agency and for which provision must be made in the community.

A participant in one of the conferences arranged by the Reconnaissance Study expressed concern regarding the identification of causative or contributing problems in the public assistance field when he said, "On a national basis we really do not know who the people are who are on assistance and what their needs are. We have some notion of the number that are disabled or handicapped, but we have no idea about how many are on relief because they are feeble-minded or have a low educational background. I would like to see something developed to tell us who these people are, whether they need psychiatric care, medical care, adult education, or something else. Then the policies that we have today could be measured against the problems that we find among the people on public assistance."

There is a tendency in a field of practice such as social work for the practitioners to be concerned with the causative or contributing problems which they can deal with through the skills and knowledge and facilities they have available. We see this tendency among librarians, to mention another field of practice, whose approach to improving international relations is apt to center on making printed matter about other nations and cultures available on as wide a scale as possible. Our public assistance spokesman, wanting to go beyond study of the kind of factors with which public assistance programs as presently constituted can deal, urged a well-rounded job of description before further ventures into prescription. Since his question was not evaluative in nature, it was set aside in the conference where he raised it, which was convened to raise *evaluative* questions.

This disposition of his question illustrates one of the major hazards of a research program which makes "evaluation" its major focus. Such a program, by devoting its attention primarily to the things that the field of practice is now doing or could readily conceive of doing, is apt to be quite circumscribed in its approach to the problems facing it. If the maximum contribution of research to an applied field is going to be realized, there has to be a willingness to recognize that the most directly applicable research is not necessarily the most productive research. There has to be acceptance of the fact that the more we know about a problem, the more successful we are apt to be in devising ways of dealing with it successfully.

In Chapter III we referred to the use of fluorine in water to diminish tooth decay. This very practical measure, which the dental profession is now trying to have introduced in all communities as a public health measure, was not discovered by setting out to find what could be put into city water systems to diminish tooth decay. It was discovered because there were researchers in dentistry who were trying to find out all they could about tooth decay, whether or not they saw an immediate relation between what they discovered and what dentists were doing in their practice. It is precisely because of the importance of developing for social work the equivalent of such measures as fluoridation of water that care must be taken to guard against relating the research only to current measures for dealing with problems. What is needed is a much wider-ranging research that can look at factors which may not even occur to social workers or which they may consider beyond their sphere of activity.

Our public assistance spokesman mentioned only two or three of the possible factors contributing to the existence of a relief load in a period of full employment—lack of education, mental deficiency, psychiatric problems. He might have enumerated other factors of a quite different order such as technological developments or racial discrimination. How can we provide that a research program in social work will consider as many relevant factors as possible?

In his introduction to Dr. Kinsey's study of sexual behavior in the human male, Dr. Alan Gregg says, "Seen from four points of the compass a great mountain may present aspects that are very different one from the other—so different that bitter disagreements can arise between those who have watched the mountain, truly and well, through all the seasons, but each from a different quarter." It is by bringing together observers who have been watching the mountain from different sides and getting them to compare and try to put together their pictures of it that all the relevant factors bearing on social work programs are going to be considered and studied.

One term used by social scientists is particularly useful in describing the way in which the relevant factors in any situation are apt to come to light: the use of different "conceptual frameworks." Our concepts, or the way we look at things, will largely determine what we see.

One of the studies concerned with juvenile delinquency which was analyzed for the Reconnaissance Study illustrates the way in which the conceptual framework of the researchers determined the way they approached their problem. The Gluecks' study started with the conceptual framework of the community. They saw juvenile delinquents, first, as they are seen through the eyes of the law, namely as young people within a specified age range who have committed an offense, have been apprehended, and have been sent to a correctional school. There are many juvenile delinquents who are not sent to correctional school, of course, but it was the correctional school group as representing the more chronic and serious offenders with whom the Gluecks were concerned.

The Gluecks recognized that even the correctional school group is made up of several subgroups which may differ from one another significantly. They therefore studied the delinquents in relation to a number of other factors, such as their home conditions, background of parents, quality of family life, relationships in school and in the community, physical health, bodily constitution, verbal and performance intelligence, character and personality structure, and dynamics of temperament. These areas of possibly important differences were suggested to them by concepts derived from social work, psychiatry, psychology, sociology, medicine, and physical anthropology.

As we have already noted, the Gluecks' study was predictive, not evaluative. They were not seeking to discover what happened as a result of a particular type of treatment program. But by suggesting new homogeneous subgroupings of children whose "presenting problem" is juvenile delinquency, they have made possible more focused experiments on the effectiveness of different types of treatment.

The goal of science is, ultimately, prediction. The goal of a field of practice is to bring about a modification of what it finds. But a field of practice can be most effective in its efforts to achieve modification if it has a fairly good description of how the "natural factors" in a situation are operating. Again returning to our lawn-growing illustration, the science of botany is concerned only with describing how grass grows. It remains for the field of horticulture, using this knowledge, to introduce elements into the grass-growing process that will result in better or more abundant grass. A great deal of experimentation will be required to determine what elements are effective. But because of the knowledge which botany now has of grass-growing processes, the experimentation can be relatively efficient. Without it it would be random and accidental.

Any efforts to evaluate a program of treatment for juvenile delinquents will be more efficient and fruitful if there is available an adequate description of the forces involved in producing the delinquency. It is for this reason that a field of practice must have a close working relationship with the sciences which are describing the phenomena with which it is dealing. The more rounded the description that is available, the more precise can the field of practice be in devising and testing measures for modifying the operation of the natural forces in a situation.

Describing and standardizing the activity.—If we are to have meaningful evaluative research it is a truism that we must have a fairly precise idea of what it is we are measuring. While this might seem to be a fairly minimum expectation to bring to any piece of evaluative research, not one of the evaluative studies analyzed dealt in any systematic way with the amount or the type of service that clients received.

Hunt explicitly excludes this step from his research on the movement scale, since he was concerned only with measuring what change, if any, occurred in clients, regardless of its cause. Some clients received five interviews, some clients one hundred. In some cases a great many specific services were provided, such as financial help, summer camp experience, help in finding housing, etc. In others practically the only service provided was casework. Hunt had good reason for excluding this step. If he had tackled it he would have had to postpone his work on developing the movement scale.

In any research which looks backward, so to speak, and seeks to find out the results of service an agency has already provided, it is almost impossible to obtain any precise description of what service the agency did provide. In contrast to the "looking backward" type of research, Fritz Redl's experimental home for disturbed children, Pioneer House, showed meticulous attention before the project was ever started to plans for analyzing and recording exactly what was done with and for each child. To be sure, there were almost twice as many adults connected with Pioneer House as there were children receiving treatment. All the adults had carefully defined roles and responsibilities, and observation and recording was a specific assignment of some of them.

No real standardizing of social work activity in relation to a group of clients can be achieved without thorough planning beforehand and conscious control and recording throughout treatment. One reason that the standardization of activity at Pioneer House was possible, it might be noted parenthetically, was a consistent theoretical orientation on the part of the director and the staff to the problem of treating disturbed children. Without such a theoretical orientation they could not have decided even what elements in the Pioneer House program were worth standardizing and controlling.

The Cambridge-Somerville Youth Study represented an experimental program where there was an opportunity to achieve some standardization of service, but where little was achieved. As Helen Witmer, in her analysis in Appendix B, describes the service provided, it was "the continued friendship and wise counsel of adults who were deeply interested in them [delinquent or potentially delinquent boys], and who could secure for them access to such community services as they required." The "continued friendship and wise counsel" ranged all the way from a big brother type of relationship to that found in fairly formal therapeutic interviews by psychiatric social workers. The problem posed by this fact in terms of research findings is stated succinctly by Witmer when she says "It seemed to us that to give a great variety of services to a great variety of people, each practitioner doing what he thinks best without reference to any commonly held body of theory, is no more a scientific experiment . . . than a medical one would be in which different kinds of medicine were given to patients suffering from different kinds of disorders by doctors who held different theories as to the causes of the illnesses."

The crucial factors, it would seem, in standardizing the activity provided by a social service program for purposes of evaluative research are (1) planning such standardization of the service before it is given, and (2) having an explicitly stated theoretical approach to the treatment program that can indicate which aspects of treatment it is important to standardize. It is, of course, possible to do gross evaluations on an ex post facto basis and such evaluations will continue, no doubt, to be done. But such research is not apt to shed much light on which factors in the service program produced results or on the way in which they operated to produce them.

Measuring the degree of change.—Devising a measuring tool is apt to be a complicated and technical task in any field, and in the field of human behavior and human adjustment it is particularly difficult. Perhaps the outstanding achievement of modern psychology is its success in developing measuring instruments which are standardized and have a known degree of reliability when applied to such complicated phenomena as intelligence and public opinion.

The movement scale for use in family service agencies developed by J. McVicker Hunt and his associates is the outstanding example in the field of social work of a measuring instrument which has been constructed in accordance with modern principles of measuring human behavior and adjustment. Hunt explicitly ruled out of the project which produced the movement scale all the other steps in evaluative research except the methodological one of measurement, and with respect to this step his work represents a landmark for research in social work.

There are two crucial factors in any measuring instrument: reliability and validity. Reliability refers to the ability of an instrument to produce the same answer, within a known amount of variation, when applied repeatedly to the same situation or to similar situations. Thus a measuring tape has reliability as long as the graduations on it are even and the person using it is able to read it accurately. Even a tape that has gone through the laundry and is considerably shrunk has reliability in the sense that it will produce the same answer time after time when used to measure objects.

Validity refers to the ability of a measuring instrument to produce answers which correspond with some known standard which is accepted and recognized by all concerned with using the measure. Our shrunken tape measure lacks validity, even though it has reliability, because what it calls an inch does not correspond with what the measuring bar in the U.S. Bureau of Standards describes as an inch.

Hunt's predecessors at the Community Service Society devised an instrument for measuring the results of casework service which had reliability but not validity. The instrument consisted of a method of scoring case records by counting the number of expressions indicating distress and the number indicating relief, putting the results into a mathematical formula, and producing what was called the distress-relief quotient. A number of different workers were asked to rate a selected group of cases using this instrument and were able to achieve a high degree of agreement in the scores they obtained. The hitch in using the instrument, however, was that workers who knew the cases did not regard all the cases which had high quotients as showing improvement, nor all the cases with low quotients as showing lack of improvement. Since the measuring scale was intended for the use of caseworkers, and since there was no more acceptable standard of what constituted improvement or lack of improvement than the opinion of workers who knew the cases, the distress-relief quotient was abandoned. The Hunt movement scale is distinguished by the fact that not only does it produce consistent results when used by trained judges, but the results obtained correspond with the judgment of competent workers who know the cases.

There are a number of special problems in arriving at a measure of the outcome of service which the research projects analyzed for the Reconnaissance Study illustrate. The question of the time of measuring results is always a troublesome one. In the Cambridge-Somerville Youth Study, adjustment of the boys was rated at the close of treatment and three years later. In the Festinger study of social interaction among housing project residents, measures were taken every two or two and a half months throughout the program, thus making possible the establishment of trends, and also permitting some appraisal to be made of the influence of particular events either in the program or in the project or community. The longer the interval between treatment and measuring results, the more opportunity there is for factors which are extraneous to treatment to enter in and modify the results. Too early a measurement, however, may reflect temporary improvement which will disappear shortly after treatment has ceased. There is no "right" time to measure results, the decision depending on the nature of the service, the problem toward which it is directed, and the kind of answer being sought through the research.

Another problem in measurement is the source material on which measurement is to be based. One of the serious limitations in the development of the Hunt movement scale is that the judges rated cases on the basis of summaries prepared by the workers who carried the cases. Conceivably, such summaries could have been slanted, albeit unconsciously. Even if full case recordings had been used, however, the fact still remains that the judges would be basing their opinion on the worker's recording of what transpired in a case, and experiments have indicated a considerable degree of "selective forgetting" in case recording. An attempt to get objective data about outcome of treatment was made by Hunt's staff, some thirty-eight cases being visited five years after closing to see how they had fared. The results of this follow-up are not yet published.

One of the measures used by the Cambridge-Somerville Youth Study was the number of times a child appeared in court or was picked up by the police. Using this measure, the Study arrived at the rather unexpected finding that more of the boys who had received counseling service were known to the juvenile court than was the case with the control group boys who had received no treatment. In an effort to get behind this rather unexpected finding the research staff analyzed the quite detailed case recordings maintained by the counselors, along with the other data on the boys, and found some types of boys did seem to be benefited. The limitation of the court appearances as a measure of the results of treatment was that, although objective, the measure was so gross as to obscure important differences among different types of boys. On the other hand, the outstanding merit of the juvenile court data was that they provided a check against too optimistic an evaluation of the project's results and probably caused a much more careful analysis of the data.

This sketchy review of the problem of measurement has several implications for a program of evaluative research in social work. First, it is clear that the technical problems involved in developing a measuring instrument require specialized personnel and call for the investment of considerable time in experimentation and validation. Hunt's work required three years. Less elaborate measuring instruments are possible, but if the quality of research on problems in social work is to be advanced significantly, more undertakings of the kind made by Hunt will be required.

Secondly, measurement can be more precise, and cross checks to validate measurements more easily established, if the research is not of the "looking backward" type, that is to say, if provision is made for obtaining measures of results before any service is given. Instead of relying on case recordings which were made for administrative and treatment purposes, it might be possible to provide for electrical recordings, or, as was done in the Cambridge-Somerville Youth Study, interviews with clients by a third person. One problem that complicates the use of various measuring devices is indicated by the last suggestion, namely, that the measuring instrument may become a new variable in the treatment program which can significantly affect the way treatment progresses.

Thirdly, and perhaps most importantly, working out measuring devices to fit the particular problem being studied is apt to be a custom job. The measuring instrument must always be designed to reflect what are believed by the investigator to be the significant problems presented by the client, the significant treatment that is provided, and the significant changes which may or may not come about through treatment. In other words, the measuring instrument must reflect the theoretical approach of the investigator. It is apt to be some time before ready-made measuring instruments are going to be available which fit the tremendous variety of problems arising in social work.

Lest the task presented by the problem of measurement have the effect of unduly discouraging those concerned with evaluative research, it is important to remember that the degree of detail and precision that is sought determines the complexity of the instrument. The records of court appearances in the Cambridge-Somerville Youth Study were very easy to obtain and proved very significant for the research. Being such a gross measure, the records could not tell much about what types of boys became involved in specific types of misconduct, but they did serve to challenge the assumption on the part of the counselors that their boys had fared better than the boys in the control group. Gross measures of this kind are exceedingly important and may well serve as the starting point for more detailed and precise measures.

Determining cause-effect relationships.—Some time ago Willard Olsen of the University of Michigan conducted some experiments on helping children who suffered from reading disabilities which illustrate what he calls the "clinical fallacy." The experimental school at the University of Michigan had been providing special tutorial and other help to children who had difficulty learning to read, and in a number of instances the children were improving. A case seemed to have been made for introducing special aids for children with reading problems.

Olsen had been conducting some experiments on child development, however, which indicated that around the age of nine or ten years, certain physiological changes occurred in children which might be associated with ability to read. An experiment was therefore set up and several children suffering from reading disabilities were given special help. Their progress was checked against the progress of another group of children with reading disabilities who received no help. The two groups of children were matched, not only in terms of chronological age, but also in terms of "growth age," as indicated by certain physiological and psychological indices. It was found that the reading disability tended to disappear among some children in both groups as soon as certain physiological changes occurred, regardless of whether special help in reading had been provided.

The experiment did not prove that special reading aids were of no use. It did prove that with some children reading disability disappeared at a certain stage in growth whether special aids were provided or not.

In social work, as in the field of education, it is very easy to make the clinical fallacy of attributing changes in clients to the services the agency has provided without a real check on whether the changes might not have occurred anyway. There is only one way of determining cause-effect relationships with any degree of reliability, and this is through the use of a "control group," that is a group which is as nearly similar as possible in all relevant respects to the group receiving help, except that it receives no help.

Of the three evaluative studies analyzed for the Reconnaissance Study only one, the Cambridge-Somerville Youth Study, used a control group design. The Gluecks' study used a control group but it was to get at predictive, not treatment, factors. Hunt made no attempt to ascertain causal relationship and so he had no occasion to set up a control group; Festinger relied on a before-and-after technique, which he recognized could not produce conclusive findings.

Witmer discounts in her analysis of the Cambridge-Somerville Youth Study the ability of the control group design to shed light on causal relationships. Her reasoning, however, goes back to the undefined and variegated treatment that the boys received, not to the control group design itself. Indeed, she acknowledges that the fact the control group showed as good a record as the treatment group forced the researchers to examine the case material more analytically than they otherwise would have.

Hans-Lukas Teuber, who participated in a follow-up on the

boys in the Cambridge-Somerville Youth Study, regards the control group as the study's most valuable feature, for all its shortcomings. In discussing the study before the Association for Research in Nervous and Mental Disease, he commented:

Before the data [about juvenile court and police appearances] from the control group had become known, all but two members of the treatment staff predicted significant success. An evaluation in the usual style, based on the counselor's own story and devoid of objective indices of altered behavior, would have resulted in merely another report on eminently successful therapy.[3]

The problems in the use of control groups for evaluative research in social work are far too complex for any adequate discussion here. Two or three particular difficulties are worth noting because they bring out the requirements in the way of both personnel and facilities for designing and carrying out research using the control group technique.

One of the basic problems in the use of a control group is matching the "treatment cases" and the "controls." Obviously cases cannot be matched so as to be identical in every respect, so some decision has to be made as to which respects are most pertinent for a particular problem. In making this decision the researcher is faced with the same task we considered under the second step in evaluative research—knowing what the factors are that influence the outcome of service. The factors seen as important will depend on the conceptual framework of the researcher. Olsen could have matched his children in any number of respects, from their socio-economic status to the color of their eyes. He selected physiological and psychological growth factors because as a psychologist he knew something

---

[3] Hans-Lukas Teuber and Edwin Powers, "Evaluating Therapy in a Delinquency Prevention Program." Paper delivered at the Annual Conference of the Association for Research in Nervous and Mental Disease, New York City, December, 1951.

about these factors and suspected they were associated with ability to read.

In social work the factors that bear on the outcome of service range from broad social and economic forces impinging on the individual to his own constitutional make-up. It is important to bring the conceptual frameworks of all the various human sciences as well as of the field of social work practice to bear on the question of which factors are most apt to influence the outcome of service in relation to particular problems. These factors can then be equated in both groups, or "neutralized," and attention focused on the effect of the specific service provided by the agency. Both the use of the conceptual frameworks of the various human sciences and the technical steps involved in group matching call for personnel who have specialized training in the human sciences and in research technique. Such personnel are not apt also to be thoroughly trained in social work. As one consultant to this study put it, it would not be either feasible or economical to try to find in one skull all the knowledge needed for research in as complex a field as social work. What is more to the point is to get together a combination of people who by pooling their knowledge can come somewhere near dealing with all the factors that are important in a particular piece of research.

A second problem to note in the use of control groups is the fact that the classical pattern of a single variable being introduced while everything else is held constant is rarely attainable in applied social research. Indeed, it is rarely attainable in any research dealing with human beings. Lawrence Henderson of Harvard University has pointed out that in medicine the scientist constantly must deal with organisms in which the parts are not only numerous but also interacting. Experimental science, such as chemistry, seeks to analyze concrete reality into relatively simple elements, but the complex reality is never describable by adding up the elements, for they exist in a complex state of interaction. Thus when one element in the blood is changed, changes are apt to occur almost simultaneously in three or four other elements which in turn affect the first element.

Dealing with a number of factors which are in a state of mutual interaction is possible only by means of certain mathematical procedures. Indeed, as Henderson comments, there is no way even to begin to think, however approximately, about quantitative relationships between a large number of mutually interacting variables, except mathematically.

In research in social work, where the presence of a number of interacting variables is the rule and not the exception, the ability to draw upon recent developments in mathematics and statistics is important if new approaches which can circumvent the limitations of past research are to be developed. Again the need is indicated for specialized personnel who in all probability cannot be expected also to have professional training in social work.

A third point in the use of control groups for research in social work needs special mention, namely, that such research usually requires access to social work operations where essential research controls can be maintained. At every step in evaluative research we see the importance of such controls. The selection of clients to be included in a study, standardizing the service that is provided them, recording what happens, and applying a measure to determine change—all require special accommodation to the requirements of the research. In addition to this, where a control group is used provision must be made for follow-up and observation of members of the control group from whom service is withheld. All this requires either service programs operated for research purposes or service programs which are willing to adjust to the requirements of research for selected portions of their case load.

This very sketchy review of the problems of establishing causal relationships has emphasized the control group technique because it has been so fruitful in other fields in correcting the "clinical fallacy" to which all fields of practice are subject. No new method of treating disease in medicine, for instance, is permitted to get into general use without several control group experiments having been run on it.

There are other less complicated and less expensive—and also less reliable—methods of getting at cause-effect relationships which have not been examined. The procedure used in Festinger's study is an example of such an approach. Gross checks on cause-effect relationships by a before-and-after approach, where carefully and systematically worked out, would provide a significant advance in most social work programs, and indeed they may be the only checks that are feasible in certain situations. Used with full awareness of their limitations such checks are valuable. Used without this awareness they may serve only to perpetuate clinical fallacies and would better be left undone.

CONCLUSION

This analysis of the logic of evaluative research, and the problems involved in carrying out such research to test any particular social work practice or program, has a number of implications which have been referred to in this chapter.

It must be clear to any reader that each practice, policy, and program cannot possibly be evaluated in accordance with the steps outlined in this chapter. The number of different types of social work programs and the tremendous number of specific policies and practices to be examined in each of these programs clearly make this impossible. Any research which takes as its starting point present practices and programs and focuses all its attention on evaluating them cannot escape this fact.

There is an alternative. The alternative is to try to see the problems confronting social work as specific instances of more general problems which confront the other professions and the human sciences. If problems in social work can be accurately "typed" and related to the problems in other fields, the work that has been done on these problems in the other fields immediately becomes available to social work. To be sure, there will be significant differences in the way a problem manifests itself in a social agency and in a school or a hospital. It is essential to identify these differences if false application of otherwise valid knowledge is to be avoided, and to do this involves an understanding of the general problem and of the problem as it appears in social work. But if research in social work were to proceed on the assumption that its problems were unique and that it had to start *de novo* each time it tackled one of them, it is probable that its problems would have disappeared or changed before research on them could have been completed.

Otto Pollak in his recent book, *Social Science and Psychotherapy for Children*, urges strongly that any social researcher called in to do research in a social agency consider as his first responsibility scrutinizing the funds of knowledge already available to him and suggesting the utilization of such knowledge.[4] His suggestions for utilization of such knowledge will be tentative, of course, and Pollack warns that the suggestions he makes in his book will require controlled observations of practical results. But the research task is tremendously narrowed when application of already validated knowledge to a particular situation is the focus of the research. There is room for a

[4] Otto Pollak and collaborators, *Social Science and Psychotherapy for Children* (New York: Russell Sage Foundation, 1952), p. 23.

great deal of this kind of research in social work, research which holds promise of producing returns in a relatively short period of time as compared with research which starts out with entirely new hypotheses.

Lest what has just been said be taken to mean that all the answers to social work problems are already available in the social sciences and only need application to social work, it should be said at once that the storehouse of knowledge about individual and social behavior in the social sciences is far from full. Neither the social sciences nor other professions can contribute much to many problems confronting social work. If work is to be done on such problems it will have to be stimulated and even sponsored by social work. But even work which starts from problems that are of unique interest to social work can proceed effectively only if it builds upon the knowledge that has already been established, which means that the research must take its place in relation to research going forward in the human sciences.

In the next chapter we will proceed to analyze in more detail the problems and the promise of a partnership between social science and research in social work.

CHAPTER V

THE RELATIONSHIP BETWEEN SOCIAL SCIENCE AND RESEARCH IN SOCIAL WELFARE

IN CONSIDERING how to bring about more extensive use of research in the field of social work, it is important to recall how young social work is as a specialized field. The Conference of Charities and Corrections, now the National Conference of Social Work, did not appear until 1872. The first professional school of social work was not launched until 1898. The American Association of Social Workers was not established until 1921. And even in this brief period the field of social work has experienced a number of stages in its development.

It would be a mistake to gear all thinking about the future role of research in social work to existing social work programs. When one looks back over the last twenty years and sees the changes in America's social work structure that have occurred, it becomes clear that any thinking about the next twenty years must be broad enough to encompass changes of comparable significance.

There is little danger that social work will become prematurely crystallized if it is problem-oriented. The danger of premature crystallization arises only if social work becomes so engrossed in refining its present practices and strengthening its present institutions that it fails to see totally new approaches to the problems with which it is dealing. The social insurance programs which are less than twenty years old represent a new and apparently successful attack on the problem of providing income to dependent persons without the threat to self esteem and social position which is such a conspicuous part of assistance programs involving the means test. There are no doubt other broad social measures waiting to be devised which will deal on a preventive and mass basis with problems which now are being handled on a remedial and individual basis.

It is particularly important that research not be restricted in its focus to the treatment or remedial aspects of social work. If research is seen primarily as a resource to which to turn for solution of problems defined by the social work practitioner or administrator, its contribution to social work will be severely limited. If, however, there is not only freedom but also responsibility for research to examine problems from every relevant perspective, then various approaches to problems confronting social work are apt to suggest themselves, ranging from broad preventive measures to improved individualized treatment services.

THE UTILITARIAN BASIS OF RESEARCH IN SOCIAL WORK

There is one aspect of research in social work which needs to be stressed if the research done is to realize its maximum usefulness for the field. This is the specific goal orientation of the research, the practical purpose which justifies its launching and continuation. William Gordon has put the matter this way: The goal of research in the field of social work is the production of knowledge; the goal of knowledge in social work is to make possible more effective policies and practices; and the goal of social work policies and practices is to realize as efficiently as possible those humanitarian objectives which the profession, the agency, and the community have set.

It may seem to be laboring the obvious to say that research in social work is to produce knowledge for the use of social work, but it is this fact which suggests the need for special research facilities for social work. The research done in a social work research program may not appear very different in its methods or subject matter from any other social research, but its goal will be different. Its goal will be to test, refine, and extend knowledge for a quite specific purpose, namely, to analyze the needs giving rise to social work programs and to make the practices and the programs of social work more efficient instruments for reaching social work goals. There may be a number of intervening links between a particular research project and the goals of social work, but the links must be traceable. Otherwise, the research is scientific research which is apt to have only incidental or accidental value for social work—it is research to push back the frontiers of knowledge, but not necessarily the frontiers of social work practice.

The above distinction is frequently phrased in terms of applied and basic research. The distinction hinges around the goals of the research, not around its subject matter or its methods. The "applied research" in the social work field is going to be pursued only so long as it seems likely to produce knowledge of use to social work in reaching its goals. "Basic research" in the social sciences will be pursued as long as it is producing new knowledge, whether or not that knowledge has some discernible and immediate relevance for social work or any other field of activity.

It is worth noting that research in social work may produce knowledge which has significance for basic theory in human behavior and human relations. This will be in a sense a by-product. The goal of the research will still be to make possible a more effective social work operation and presumably will cease when it no longer advances this purpose.

THE TWO-WAY ORIENTATION OF RESEARCH IN SOCIAL
WELFARE

Research in social work has to face in two directions. It has
to face toward the goals of social welfare, including the existing and potential devices for reaching these goals. It has also to
face toward the knowledge that is available about man and
society, much of which is relevant for reaching social work
goals even though it was not developed for that purpose. These
two orientations require special skills and knowledge in any
social work research program.

The orientation toward the goals of social work requires a
substantial amount of knowledge of the development and
present operation of social work programs. It requires, indeed,
identification with the social work profession in the sense of
accepting its ethical norms and its fundamental objectives. This
orientation is acquired most directly through professional training in social work, but professional training is not the only way
to acquire it. Indeed, it is no guarantee in itself that it has been
acquired. Some of social work's most prominent leaders have
not come up through professional training, and there are products of professional training who seem to have little understanding and acceptance of social work's goals and values as
they have emerged historically. However it may have been
acquired, there must be knowledge of social work programs
and practice and acceptance of its goals in any research program
in social work. This is not to say that every person in a social
work research program must have this background. It is to say
that the background would have to be adequately represented
in one or more persons involved in the planning and execution
of social work research.

The orientation toward the available knowledge of man
and society requires another kind of background. Such knowl-

edge is to be found in a number of sciences and professional fields. Knowledge of human behavior and human relations, like most other knowledge, has been derived two ways—empirically and, for want of a better term, theoretically. That is to say, much of the information about human behavior and human relations that is put to effective use every day has been derived from the practical experience and observations of persons working with people. And on the other hand, there is some knowledge about human behavior and human relations that has been derived through systematic investigation of hypotheses which has led to generalizations and new hypotheses which have required additional investigation and testing—this is the way of science.

THE WAYS KNOWLEDGE IS DEVELOPED

When we look at the whole field of human relations and see the knowledge that is available, we cannot but be struck with what a large proportion of it is empirical and how little, relatively, has been contributed up to this point through theoretically based investigations. This is particularly striking when we compare the status of our knowledge about people with the status of our knowledge about things. In the world of things the knowledge that has been acquired through the procedures of theory-based scientific investigation has long since matched in practical usefulness that which has been learned empirically. Atomic fission, with all its potential for the improvement or destruction of mankind, is only the most recent example of knowledge which has been made possible by the procedures of science and which in all likelihood would never have been discovered through common sense, trial-and-error approaches.

There has been increasing optimism in recent years about the potential contribution of theoretical science to the field of human behavior and human relations. Stuart Chase's book *The Proper Study of Mankind* is a recent popular statement of this potential contribution. It should not be too discouraging to note how limited the contributions of the social sciences have been up to this point, when their brief history is considered. In spite of the relative youth of the social sciences, their potential contribution has been demonstrated clearly through the application of knowledge derived scientifically in solving many problems such as handling mixed Negro and white units in World War II, selecting pilots for the Air Force, conducting public opinion polls, treating psychotic patients, training mentally deficient persons, and many other things.

Up to the present time there is very little to point to in the way of knowledge on which social work relies that has been contributed through the characteristic approach of science— application of theory to a given set of phenomena, systematic testing to determine the extent to which the theory is able to account for the relationships observed, and the formulation of new theory which in turn will require testing and restatement. How to relate the insights and understanding of social work to the body of theory which has developed and is continuing to develop in the behavior sciences is indeed difficult. There are some who hold that social work will be held back in developing knowledge which is useful in achieving its goals if it tries to relate its research to the theoretical formulations of the social sciences. They contend that social work, because of its intimate experience with the problems of individuals and groups, its description of these problems in terms of their causes and their probable response to treatment, and its integration of several variables into general statements of principle governing diagnosis and treatment, is further ahead than the social sciences in understanding human behavior and its probable responses to treatment.

THE APPROACH OF SCIENCE TO DEVELOPING KNOWLEDGE

There is another point of view as to the most efficient way by which research can develop the knowledge required to deal with the problems encountered in social work programs. It is the point of view on which the recommendations in this report rest, namely, that research in social work must be vitally related to the more basic scientific research going forward in the field of human behavior and human relations. The reasons for this point of view will be stated shortly. But it is worth stressing first that to urge social work research to build upon and to make use of research in the social sciences in no sense should be taken as a recommendation that social work abdicate responsibility for developing its own research activities or for developing new concepts out of the materials with which it deals. Such a disclaimer may appear unnecessary, and perhaps it is. But there is already a considerable body of opinion which holds that building research activity in social work on the concepts and research methods of the social sciences represents an abdication of social work's responsibility for formulating and improving its own principles and practice. One of the reasons for this attitude is probably the fact that there are few persons who have contributed to the development of the body of social work knowledge as it exists today who have the background to restate this knowledge and relate it to concepts in the social sciences. For persons without such background who are not willing to acquire it, relating social work research to social science theory does involve abdication of responsibility for research to others who are so equipped. There are, however, an increasing, though still small, number of persons in social work who have background and versatility in social science research. The recommendations in this report rest upon the expectation that there will be even more such persons.

To return to the reasons for the recommendation of this report that research directed toward the problems in social work be related to the knowledge of human behavior and human relations as developed in the social sciences: The first reason is that the tremendous advances in knowledge that have occurred in modern times are due to the procedures of scientific research. Since the time when some prehistoric genius stumbled onto the principle of the wheel, man has always shown considerable ability to learn from observation and experience and considerable ingenuity in developing new ways of dealing with his problems. During the past three hundred years, however, progress in understanding and mastering nature through scientific research has gone forward so rapidly that more has been accomplished than in all the preceding centuries. The explanation of this fact seems to rest in the vastly more efficient approach to problem solution represented by theoretically oriented scientific research as compared with crude empirical, trial-and-error approaches.

James Bryant Conant suggests the analogy of the spectrum to illustrate the respective contributions of theoretically oriented and of trial-and-error, or what he calls "empirical," research. He writes:

At one end [of the spectrum] we may place the changing conceptual schemes arising from experiment and giving rise to experiment—pure science if you will. At the other end we place the improvements in the practical arts of industry and agriculture that have been going on for milleniums. Not until about 1600 does the pure science end of the spectrum become visible. While this end increases in width and intensity for the next two hundred years, so likewise, the opposite end continues to glow brightly. Then the intervening space narrows and in this century the intermediate zone becomes full of glowing lines connecting the once totally disparate ends with each other.
. . . Although we can still recognize the two ends of the spec-

trum to which I have referred, the intermediary zone now occupies the main position, for not only has pure science invaded the practical arts, but the practical arts have penetrated deeply into science. In many areas one cannot distinguish between the techniques of the scientists interested only in new conceptual schemes, and those of the experimenter interested only in new industrial machines or processes.

. . . .

It seems to me that it may be of use to the layman in trying to untangle the complexities of the present situation to have in mind this spectral analogy and to take the two opposite extremes as points of reference. One may then try to locate a given problem on the spectrum. The nearer the point to the empirical end, the greater the degree of empiricism now present. Or to put it another way, we may define the degree of empiricism in a given area as the degree to which progress now depends merely on learning through doing things, trial and error, by repeated attempts to do things without any embracing conceptual scheme or new concepts to steer the way.[1]

In suggesting the analogy of the spectrum, Dr. Conant was seeking to clarify the respective roles of theoretically oriented and "empirical" or trial-and-error research in industry and medicine. It takes a considerable leap to apply the analogy to the field of human behavior and human relations, largely because the conceptual end of the spectrum is so undeveloped in the social sciences as compared with the natural sciences. The *pattern* of relationship between theoretical and empirical approaches to problems, however, remains the same, and it seems reasonable to suppose that progress in the social as well as in the physical and biological fields will be advanced through the interpenetration of these two approaches.

At any rate, it would take a bold prophet to assert that re-

[1] James Bryant Conant, "The Inter-Relation of Pure and Applied Science in the Field of Medicine," *Perspectives in Medicine* (New York: Columbia University Press, 1949), pp. 137–38.

search in social work should proceed independently without seeking to relate its insights to the still fragmentary but growing body of theory in the social sciences. The burden of proof would seem to rest on the advocates of such an approach, since it departs from the pattern which has proved so fruitful in the solution of problems in industry, medicine, and many other fields.

The second reason why social work should seek to relate its knowledge to the social sciences is that it thereby obtains more reliable access to the knowledge of other professions working in the field of human relations. There is increasing interest in such fields as education, industrial management, and counseling in stating the problems and principles of these fields in terms which can be related to the thinking being done in the social sciences. As social work states its insights and its procedures in these terms also it will be in touch with the work that is going on in a much broader field of practice in human relations.

Social work has demonstrated in the past a lively interest in tapping the knowledge and experience of other fields of practice, notably psychiatry. It has not been as sophisticated as it might have been, however, in assessing the extent to which generalizations in these other fields have been subjected to the verification which is characteristic of science. Consequently it has sometimes seized upon a possible explanation of the dynamics involved in a particular situation as a valid description of fact and has stressed the psychological factors operating in the situation to the exclusion of other equally significant factors. The danger of what may be called empirical borrowing from other fields of practice is reduced when the borrowing is done with at least some awareness of the extent to which the knowledge or technique borrowed has been tested through the methods and in relation to the concepts of the relevant sciences. It is the promise of access to a wider body of thinking and experimentation in the field of human behavior and human relations which provides the second reason for the recommendation in this report that research in social work be vitally related to research in the social sciences.

The third reason for recommending a vital relationship to research in the social sciences is the contribution of the social sciences in the form of research tools. Scientific research by its nature has had to devote a great deal of attention to developing research methods and tools appropriate to the materials with which it is dealing. Research in social work has already borrowed such research techniques as sampling, measurement of mental abilities, and opinion polling, and can be expected to borrow more extensively as research activity is expanded.

While few instances can be found in the field of human relations where the contributions of theory to the solution of problems in practice have been of the same order as occurs in the natural sciences, there is a more limited kind of contribution which social science theory has made. This is to suggest some of the possibly relevant factors operating in a situation, even though an integrated theory as to the way they are operating has not been evolved. Robert Merton refers to this when he speaks of social science suggesting "overlooked variables" which should be taken into account. There are a number of distinctive perspectives that have been cultivated in the various branches of social science which are apt to be suggestive for even empirical research undertakings in social work.

THE CONTRIBUTION OF SOCIAL WORK TO SOCIAL SCIENCE

The emphasis in this chapter has been on the contribution of social science to research in social work. It reflects the purpose of this report to improve research in social work. It would be unfortunate if this emphasis served to obscure the other kind of contribution which should come out of a close working relationship between social science and research in social work, namely, the contribution of social work research to social science.

When we consider the way in which other fields of practice have been able to contribute in quite fundamental ways to the sciences to which they are related, we can see the importance of not overlooking this possibility in the field of social work. In general, social work is concerned with dysfunction in society, with the breakdown of "normal" functioning. It is a commonplace that some of the most important clues to normal functioning in the biological or physical sciences have come through the study of malfunction. It is reasonable to expect that the breakdown of normal functioning which precipitates the need for social work services will shed light on the operation of individual and social forces that operate to produce normal functioning.

There is another characteristic of a field of practice such as social work which makes possible significant contributions to science, namely, the fact that a field of practice undertakes to intervene in the natural course of events, thereby producing changes which can be observed and analyzed. Frequently the kind of intervention which is possible as part of a social work program would never be possible through scientific experiment. Take as one example the effect on business conditions of the income maintenance programs provided in the Social Security Act. How could even the most ambitious economic research hope to achieve experimentally what the Social Security Act achieved through legislative enactment?

Unfortunately, there are very few examples of the way experience accumulated in the operation of social work programs has been utilized to test or to extend social science knowledge. This is due, no doubt, to a lack of communication between the fields of social science research and social work practice. This lack of communication is part of the larger problem of maintaining liaison between the social sciences and the professions which work in the field of human relations. As progress is made on this larger problem through the work of such organizations as the Russell Sage Foundation and the National Institute of Mental Health, ways should emerge by which research in social work and the social sciences can be more closely related.

In this chapter we have considered some of the problems and some of the possibilities in a closer working relationship between the field of social work practice and the social sciences. In the next chapter we will examine some of the practical alternatives for achieving this relationship.

CHAPTER VI

THE ADMINISTRATIVE SETTING
FOR RESEARCH IN SOCIAL WORK

WE COME now to the question of where to locate research
activity in social work. There are a limited number of possibilities we have to consider. They are as follows:
A. Research units in social work agencies
   1. In single agencies
   2. In councils of social agencies and public welfare de-
      partments
B. Research units in universities
   1. In schools of social work
   2. In social science departments
   3. In social research laboratories
C. Independent research units
   1. Foundation research programs
   2. Private research enterprises
There is, of course, the individual investigator who is going to
conduct his research wherever he finds himself—in a university,
an agency, or as free-lance researcher. We are concerned here,
however, with the research enterprise which, because of its
size and character, requires some kind of institutional structure.

CRITERIA FOR A CONTINUING PROGRAM OF RESEARCH IN
SOCIAL WORK

Our analysis up to this point has suggested certain elements which should be provided in any structure for a continuing program of research in social work.

1. There should be a knowledge of social work theory and practice and an intimate awareness of the problems confronting social work on which research is needed.

2. There should be a working knowledge of the body of scientific theory which has relevance for social work and which is found in such sciences as sociology, psychology, social psychology, anthropology, economics, and political science.

3. There should be technical skill in organizing and carrying out "applied" research.

4. There should be sufficient size to a research unit so that the benefits of teamwork among scientists and practitioners and among different kinds of scientists can be realized.

5. There should be assurance of continuity in a research program to make possible recruitment of qualified staff and to put research on a program rather than project basis.

6. There should be freedom for the research to go where the evidence leads it and freedom to publish findings, even when they are painful to a particular group.

7. There should be access to experimental social work operations where the research objective is paramount to the service objective.

8. There should be provision for continuing interaction between the research unit and practitioners and administrators in social work so that the research will be responsive to the needs of social work programs and so that research findings can be incorporated into policy making and practice.

These eight elements are apt to be present in greater or lesser degree in the different types of research units which we have identified. The research unit which is associated with a graduate professional school of social work in a university, however, is the type of unit recommended in this report as making the most adequate provision for the eight elements listed.

Before examining in some detail this type of unit, let us scan briefly the advantages and limitations of the other types of units.

RESEARCH UNITS IN SOCIAL WORK AGENCIES

There have been some notable research programs in individual agencies—to mention only two: the work of Healy and Bronner at the Judge Baker Child Guidance Center in Boston and the work of Hunt at the Community Service Society of New York City. These units have certainly had an intimate awareness of problems needing research in their own agencies. They have tended, possibly because of their size, to draw mainly on one field such as psychiatry, sociology, or psychology. Their work has had continuity and has been cumulative, on the whole. They have been able to maintain laboratory controls over certain aspects of the operating programs with which they have been affiliated. There appears to have been freedom for the research in many respects, but limitation in others. A limitation noted in one unit particularly was a reluctance in the agency to extend inquiries to problems regarded as important by the researcher, but regarded by the administrator or practitioner as too threatening, too far-removed from day-by-day practice, or as requiring too much interference with agency operation. The extent to which research findings have been used in policy making and practice has varied, it appears. In general it would be reasonable to expect more readiness on the part of agencies to use research findings for which they have spent money than to use research done outside the agency.

The bulk of research in social work today is located in state and federal public welfare departments and in the councils of social agencies in large cities. Typically this research is strictly operational in character, that is to say, it is undertaken to provide answers to specific questions raised by administrative and policy-forming personnel. The major activity of such research units is usually the collection and analysis of data on program operations, such data being essential to the budgeting activity of any community chest or state welfare department.

Research units of this type have many of the same assets and limitations as have research units in individual agencies. One of their important strengths is apt to be an intimate knowledge of the social work programs with which they work and the problems facing them. Because their personnel are so operations-oriented, however, they are apt to see problems primarily in terms of the policies and services of their agencies and to overlook the variables and the alternatives which would occur to more broadly oriented researchers.

A special hazard to a research program which is located in a governmental agency is pointed out in a memorandum published by the faculty of the University of Toronto School of Social Work:

A . . . factor which limits the work of any governmental research unit is that of departmental jurisdiction. For example, unemployment insurance is a field which comes within the concern of the Department of Labor. Therefore, the Research Division of the Department of National Health and Welfare does not normally feel free to investigate problems of unemployment insurance even though these may be very closely related to those of other branches of social security with which the Department is concerned.[1]

In 1944 in Michigan when some studies on services for children were being conducted in connection with the Governor's

[1] School of Social Work, University of Toronto, *Research in Social Welfare* (Toronto, 1951; mimeograph), p. 13.

Youth Guidance Program, the personal leadership of the Governor was required to bring about a unified treatment of data which were scattered throughout several state departments, including welfare, mental health, public instruction, corrections, and state police. Such problems as this are not insuperable, but they tend to place artificial limits on the scope of a public welfare research unit's inquiries.

In councils of social agencies the fact that the research function is so closely related to the disbursal of funds adds a serious complication to the conduct of research in cooperation with agencies.

Two special problems affecting research located in operating agencies or councils of social agencies were pointed out by Robert Merton in one of the conferences sponsored by the Reconnaissance Study. One problem is that the activities of the researcher tend to be turned into advice-giving instead of research. What is wanted by the administrator is answers and suggestions. Research takes time, and policy needs to be formed now, so the researcher functions as a consultant, drawing on his theoretical and practical knowledge. While this is a valuable service, it is not research.

Another problem arises from the fact that the position of a researcher in an agency is necessarily subordinate to that of the chief of the operating organization. It is difficult for him to turn down requests, even though he questions whether a particular problem is susceptible of research, or feels that an additional research undertaking will interfere with successful prosecution of existing projects. The *ad hoc* researcher attached to an agency for a special assignment has a status and an independence which a staff person is apt to have difficulty in maintaining.

A third limitation of agency-based research is that a premium tends to be put on findings of immediate importance for policy making and practice and the methodological and theoretical by-products of the research tend to be neglected. Dorwin Cart-wright has pointed this out in an analysis of the use of social psychologists in commercial public opinion polling organizations, where the goal is quick and economical delivery of an answer to a client in terms that are understandable to him. "People who want to complicate the research report . . . with data whose relation to a conceptual system may be clear but which have no superficial relation to the problem . . . have found it hard to work in many research organizations devoted exclusively to applied research." [2]

Stress has been placed in the section above on the limitations peculiar to research units located in operating agencies. This is to bring out for the reader the reason why the Reconnaissance Study is recommending a unit located in a graduate school of social work. A balanced treatment would permit a longer listing of the special assets of a unit located within operating agencies or councils of agencies.

RESEARCH UNITS IN SOCIAL SCIENCE DEPARTMENTS OF
UNIVERSITIES

The research conducted in social science departments in universities reflects the interests and background of faculty members in these departments, and this is as it should be. During the depression, when unemployment and its accompanying problems was a major concern of the whole community, many social scientists conducted studies bearing directly on public welfare programs. Today, research related to the planning and operation of social work programs does not constitute a major concern of any social science department in Michigan. With

[2] Dorwin Cartwright, "Basic and Applied Social Psychology," *Philosophy of Science*, XVI, No. 3 (July, 1949), p. 205.

social work only one of a great number of fields for applied social research, it is unlikely that the social science departments will meet the essential requirement of a concern with social work and an intimate knowledge of its problems.

It would seem reasonable to expect that the contribution of social science departments to research in social work will be on an *ad hoc* basis, as particular problems are defined and special research projects set up.

Since World War II there has been a tremendous expansion of university-related social research laboratories which are variously labeled institutes, bureaus, and committees. One of the best known is the Institute for Social Research at the University of Michigan. How adequately can such units provide the eight elements we have identified as important for research in social work?

There is not at present any special knowledge of social work and its problems in these laboratories, but this is true initially of many other areas in which such laboratories do research. Staff members are employed by these laboratories who can supply the special knowledge required for a particular project. The contributions of the laboratory are experience in the art of planning and carrying out social research in an applied setting, an interdisciplinary team of scientists who can bring the relevant concepts in their respective disciplines to bear on a problem, and skill in the use of various research tools. Most laboratories of this type depend to a considerable extent on income from research contracts. The subject matter studied is dependent to a considerable extent, therefore, on what people are willing to pay for.

In respect to most of the elements in a continuing program of research in social work the social research laboratories measure up, or could measure up given adequate and continuing financial support for such research. The basic question that has to be asked is "can the scientific research for a professional field such as social work be developed by buying it on a contract basis from a social research laboratory?"

When the question is asked this way, most people will agree the answer is "no." Early in this study we confronted the fact that "evaluative" research was possible only as fundamental research on social work problems and processes was undertaken. Stress has been placed on the contribution to social work principles and practice which may be expected from a systematic translation, application, and testing of concepts developed in the basic sciences. The goal of this activity is not simply the answering of a series of questions or problems, but the development of broad principles for application in the day-by-day practice of the profession.

How is this goal most likely to be realized? It seems reasonable to assume that it will be realized as the result of persistent, continuous effort by those who have made the field of social work—specifically, research in social work—their major concern. Unfortunately, the supply of persons with training in the social sciences and for whom the field of social work is their major concern is limited. The long-range solution to research in social work is to expand the supply of such persons. Contract research, meanwhile, provides an immediate resource for getting work done on specific problems in social work.

INDEPENDENT RESEARCH UNITS

There is no major foundation in the country today which operates a research unit concerned exclusively, or even primarily, with social work. Until such a foundation, indeed until a number of such foundations, are available, we cannot look to research units operated by foundations to carry major responsibility for the conduct of research in this field. Most of the foundations do not operate research programs at all, preferring to give financial support to research which may be located in universities or research organizations or which may be conducted independently by individual investigators.

In another field, medicine, a large foundation set up and operated a research program, independent of universities or hospitals, which has made a significant impact on medical research—the Rockefeller Institute for Medical Research. A similar operation in the field of social work could provide, by virtue of its financial resources and its specific focus on social work, all eight elements we have outlined as essential for a program of research in social work. The trend in foundations, however, is away from such projects. They prefer to support activities which are part of ongoing programs and which have some prospect of continuing after the foundation diminishes or withdraws its support.

Turning to private research organizations, we do not find many of them in social work. Usually they are set up to provide a vehicle for one or two researchers to carry on research on a contract basis for agencies or foundations. Such enterprises have all the limitations of the social research laboratories connected with universities and few of their advantages.

RESEARCH UNITS IN PROFESSIONAL SCHOOLS OF SOCIAL
WORK

We come now to the research unit which is located in a graduate professional school of social work in a university. To simplify reference to it in the following discussion we will call it an institute for research in social work, or simply an institute. As conceived here the institute would be closely integrated with the teaching program of the school so that it could provide a laboratory to train students specializing in research and could strengthen the research emphasis in the whole curriculum. At the same time a certain degree of independence would be provided so that it could exercise final determination on matters of research policy and procedure. This would include final determination as to what research would be undertaken and in what sequence.

How does, or rather how could, an institute for research in social work located in a professional social work school and staffed by social workers and social scientists measure up to the eight criteria we have listed for evaluating a research program?

1. *Knowledge of the field of social work.*—Location in a professional school of social work should tend to keep the institute identified with social work practice and aware of the problems in that field. As has been pointed out before, it is important that the scientifically oriented research program operating in a professional field be able to approach the problems of the professional field, not simply from the perspective of science, but from the perspective of the administrator or practitioner. Unless the research program can maintain this perspective, it may redefine problems of practice for research purposes in such a way as to destroy their relevance for the field of practice. Two considerations must always enter into the selection of a problem for research in an applied field—its relevance and its susceptibility of research. If a research program is to be able to make its own determination as to both these factors it must have the perspective of the field of practice as well as of science. To have the research unit a part of a professional school which is concerned day by day with the practice of social work is one way of keeping it constantly aware of the perspective of the field of practice.

2. *Use of social science concepts and research procedures.*— The location of an institute for research in social work in a

university is most crucial in relation to personnel. Although social scientists have been appearing increasingly in positions in government and industry, particularly since World War II, the natural habitat of the social scientist is still the university. The career line of a psychologist or sociologist or anthropologist is fairly clearly defined as long as he remains in an academic setting. Outside this setting he is pioneering, and his status, his financial security, and his road to professional advancement is at risk. Several of the scientists who have ventured into applied research in social work have kept one anchor to windward in the form of part-time teaching and have returned to university positions after a time. Even appointment to the faculty of a school of social work represents a departure from the well-defined career line of a social scientist, and special inducements to justify such a departure will no doubt be required if top-notch personnel are to be obtained. One commonly used device for maintaining a scientist's relationship with his own science while working in an applied field in a university is that of the dual appointment, that is, appointment to a professional school and to an academic department. The dual appointment arrangement has two special merits. First, the scientist in an applied setting can serve as a means of transmitting to his colleagues in the basic sciences the theoretical problems which are impeding the developments in the applied field with which he is concerned. Secondly, the liaison with operating programs provided by a scientist working within an applied field opens up new settings which are amenable to research controls for the conduct of basic research.

An advantage of the institute which is located in a professional school over a unit in one of the social science departments is the opportunity afforded for development of an interdisciplinary team of scientists. The focal center in an applied field is the problems of the applied field, which always cut across the boundaries of the individual sciences. In a social science department, the focus is appropriately on the problems of theory extension in the particular science or on the application of theory in the science to practical situations. An interdisciplinary approach is not excluded, of course, in a university where social science departments are closely integrated.

3. *Skill in carrying out applied research.*—While it is possible to overdo the distinction between so-called applied and basic research, there are differences in the approach and goals of these two types of research which call for different capabilities on the part of the researcher. The Bureau of Applied Social Research at Columbia University is currently engaged in developing a curriculum and special case materials for training applied social researchers. The Columbia project rests on the proposition that applied research, like any applied field, is an art as well as a science.

One qualification which is required for research in an applied field like social work is an understanding of, and an ability to work in relation to, fairly large-scale administrative frameworks such as are found in state welfare departments, councils of social agencies, or large private agencies. There is need also for skill in interpreting research work to people without a research background; for patience and skill in working with committees; for ability to develop estimates on the time and cost of applied research projects; for ability to organize, train, and supervise staff; for skill in presenting materials for the different publics interested in research findings, and this means in addition to preparation of a readable final report, a continuing "feed-back" process which gets the research into the life stream of the consumer group.

The research man in an applied research unit functions as a team member both in the selection and formulation of problems and in carrying through the research. This means that not all good social scientists will also make good staff members of a research unit of the kind here proposed. Special qualifications in the area of interpersonal relations and in planning and administration are needed. It is particularly important that the director of the research unit have skill in planning and directing research in an applied setting.

4. *Adequacy of size of unit.*—Size may seem a rather mechanical criterion for a research institute in social work but creation of a unit of four to seven professional staff members supplemented by graduate assistants and clerical workers would provide one of the most important departures from the prevailing pattern of research in social work. The concept of interdisciplinary research itself suggests a unit large enough to provide for representation, probably in some combination, of such sciences as sociology, social psychology, psychology, and anthropology, on the one hand, and economics, history, and political science, on the other.

It is not simply the wider range of knowledge represented in a research group of four to seven persons which makes the factor of size important. Just as important is the kind of interaction that takes place in a group. Rensis Likert has commented that two researchers are three times as good as one, and that three researchers are four times as good as two. Size makes a qualitative difference.

To stress the advantages of group research is not in any way to discount the contribution of the lone investigator working on a modest scale. He will probably continue to be the backbone of scientific research, as he has been in the past. Donald Young and Paul Webbink have pointed out that the primary purpose of a research organization is to supplement, rather than supplant, individual effort.

5. *Continuity for the research.*—Applied research in social work is frequently of the fire-fighting variety which adds little

to the body of general knowledge that can be used in social work practice and administration. If research is to be cumulative, and if some of the more difficult problems are to be tackled for which special research tools and methods need to be developed, then there must be provision for long-range planning of research.

It is difficult to make adequate provision in any applied research organization for initial planning activity and for periodic stock-taking and adjustment of plans. Pressure for getting important projects launched is hard to resist, and the fact that the planning task is difficult and encumbered with numerous imponderables does not make it any easier for the researcher to stay with this phase of the job. In a venture of the kind proposed here, however, there must be staff time available for the planning, or better, programming, of research.

In an institute for research in social work, it is assumed that a considerable portion of the financial support will come from research contracts with agencies, once the program is established and operating. Contract research presents both opportunities and hazards. It permits access to data not otherwise accessible and to a ready-made avenue for transmission of findings. At the same time it involves undertaking work on problems for which agencies are willing to spend money, adherence to projected timetables, and production of answers of immediate and practical use to the agency paying for the research.

If too large a proportion of the resources of a research unit have to go for this type of research, the contribution of the unit to the testing and extension of the body of knowledge of social work practice and administration will be limited. What is called for is a basic general research budget to which the contract research represents a useful extension. All social research laboratories have such a budget, but all of them would like it to be larger.

It is characteristic of consumers of applied research to conceive of research as a series of projects, each one of which is fairly complete in itself. Scientific research is not carried on in this way. The typical pattern is for an investigator to work in a particular area over a period of years and to come up from time to time with reports on specific findings emerging from his experiments. These reports do not represent completion of the research, but bench marks in its progress. It is inevitable that this is so when fundamental, as contrasted with immediate or operational, problems are dealt with.

One of the devices for protecting fundamental research work from the kind of pressures described above is to make specific provision in a research organization for handling the short-run, practically oriented type of research. This research will be better done because of its relationship to a more fundamental research program, and it will absorb the pressure for immediately useful, operationally oriented research activity.

6. *Freedom for the research.*—It is the universal experience of social researchers working in an applied field that there are certain sensitive areas where freedom to explore and to inquire encounters restrictions. When an agency's sources of financial support, its relationships with its clientele, its standing in the community, are threatened, its will to survive is apt to prevail over its devotion to science. Not only the agency, but also the practitioner whose career has been bound up with certain presuppositions about practice—both are apt to be reluctant to examine the basic assumptions on which they have operated. This attitude on the part of agencies and individuals is inevitable and must be respected and accommodated in every way possible. The final decision as to where an inquiry must go, however, will have to rest with the researcher if he is to remain accountable for the integrity of the research. Locating a research program in a university, where the independence of research is

well fortified, is one of the ways by which freedom in carrying out and publishing research can be protected.

It is not only freedom from pressures connected with institutional or professional self-interest which is important. Just as important is freedom from pressures on the time and energy of the researcher to undertake teaching and administrative or community responsibilities. Monastic seclusion is not being recommended here, but an institute where research responsibilities are primary and teaching responsibilities incidental should minimize the diversions which so often hinder the researcher in an academic institution. Donald Young and Paul Webbink, in discussing this problem, have said, "There are many barriers to the conduct of research by social scientists who earn their living as members of educational faculties. . . . The fundamental problem is not so much financial as cultural; it is an aspect of the prevailing pattern of academic life and work. There is too great a tendency to regard research as a leisure-time activity and too much interference with research interests by other duties with a higher priority, to encourage scientific investigation by faculty personnel or to permit the degree of application and continuity which is imperative." [3]

Freedom of publication is so fundamental for research that it should be possible to take it for granted. This is not the case. Philip Klein, who has had a long and distinguished career in doing research for agencies and organizations in social work, has stated that a major obstacle to research progress in social work is the proprietary attitude which agencies have held toward research which they have sponsored. He urges that researchers avoid undertaking any research which cannot be published and shared with the profession.[4] With the need for

[3] Donald Young and Paul Webbink, in *Items,* publication of the Social Science Research Council, I, No. 3 (September, 1947), p. 2.
[4] Philip Klein, "Past and Future in Social Welfare Research," *The Social Welfare Forum, 1951* (New York: Columbia University Press, 1951), p. 146.

research so far in excess of the resources for doing it, Dr. Klein's recommendation seems a reasonable minimum to which any university-related institute for research in social work should adhere.

7. *Experimental social work operations.*—Special agencies or units of agencies in social work are needed where the research objective is paramount over the service objective. Research is complex enough on such phenomena as social services without increasing the complexity by introducing all the special variables that are found in any operating social work program. Consider a few obvious controls which can be exercised in a research-focused agency or unit: control of intake, of staff selection, and of giving and withholding specific services. With these factors subject to control by the researcher, the task of designing an experiment becomes much simpler; indeed, it becomes possible for the first time.

Fritz Redl, who set up Pioneer House in Detroit to provide an opportunity for observation of the behavior of disturbed children and their response to treatment, has stated graphically the need for the laboratory type of agency. He says, "We must be as careful with respect to our psychological 'atmosphere' as medical science has learned to be with the biotic atmosphere in which certain of its operations are to be carried out. No surgery can be successful if, at the same time, free passage is given to germ invasion which will then cause death from sepsis even if a diseased organ is removed successfully. Similarly, no attempts at influencing behavior pathology can be successful if, at the same time, every part of the environment is not kept scrupulously 'clean' from the point of view of psychological hygiene." [5] And, he might have gone on, no conclusions can be drawn as to the efficacy of attempts to influence behavior

[5] Fritz Redl, *Children Who Hate* (Glencoe, Illinois: The Free Press, 1951), p. 35.

pathology if other significant influences have been operating unnoted and uncontrolled.

The need for, and appropriateness of, an experimental agency or unit will vary depending upon the type of problem under study. Various types of experimental units are possible, ranging from a residential treatment home to simply a selected case load in an agency. Provision of experimental facilities should not be as difficult as might be assumed at first. It would be reasonable to expect that services in existing agencies could be carried on with the regular cost of the services met by the agencies, and that only the additional costs entailed by the research requirements would have to be met out of special funds. Teaching and research hospitals operate this way, and there is already in social work a precedent for this sort of thing in the pattern of field work training in agencies for students in schools of social work.

8. *Interaction between research and practice.*—We have noted that protection of research from pressures originating in the field of social work operations is important, but just as important is responsiveness to the needs and the points of view of practitioners and administrators. This is particularly vital at the point of problem formulation, as we have observed, and communication of research findings.

Applied research implies knowledge of the field of application as well as of research procedures. Particularly in setting up experimental situations where research is to be done on practice, there is no substitute for the knowledge in the field of practice as to what is possible, what the hazards are, and what practical measures are available to bring program operations into line with the requirements of research.

Communication of research findings to agencies and practitioners and also to the field of social work education is a task that has many aspects. It is important, of course, to use the right words and to start off with the practitioner group at the point of its interest and understanding. It is perhaps just as important that new ideas about theory and practice come from within the field of social work. It is probably characteristic of any field, and it certainly is of social work, that counsel coming from the outside is much slower to penetrate and to become accepted than is counsel from within the field. We can anticipate that much of what is said about social work practice in a research program of the kind here proposed will run counter to existing assumptions and will encounter resistance, even under the best of circumstances. This resistance will simply be accentuated if the counsel comes from a source which is not regarded as identified with the objectives of the profession and its ethical norms.

The most fundamental contribution of a research program, and one that will require more than good communication if it is to get across, will be the *approach* which it brings to practice and administration, rather than the findings coming out of specific researches. Social work education has, over the past thirty years, been so absorbed in transmitting principles and concepts and developing practitioner skills that it has not given adequate attention to developing an awareness on the part of the student of the basis for the concepts and practices he is being taught. Yet an awareness of this basis is essential for a continuing modification and extension of concepts and practices throughout a professional career. To infuse the graduate professional curriculum in social work with the attitudes of science toward the testing and verification of knowledge would be to realize communication between research and practice of the most far-reaching and fundamental character. With the establishment of a common perspective between researcher and practitioner, the transmission of specific findings emerging from research would be vastly facilitated.

Such a development cannot occur over a short period of time and will have to take place in a number of schools of social work to be effective. But there is ample evidence that the research approach to testing and developing social work knowledge is receiving increased attention in leading schools of social work throughout the country. It may well be that this development will be the outstanding characteristic of social work education during the next twenty-five years. Something very close to this was suggested by Gordon Hamilton in the concluding paragraph of her address to the American Association of Schools of Social Work in 1949, where she said, "Cross-fertilization between the social sciences and the broad field of welfare practice is probably the most important goal for the future of professional education and for the profession as a whole." [6]

CONCLUSION

This review of the advantages and limitations of the various locations for research in social work has brought out the major considerations which have led to the recommendation that an institute for research in social work be established as part of a graduate professional school of social work in a university. In the next chapter we turn to the practical problems in implementing this recommendation.

[6] Gordon Hamilton, "The Inter-action of School and Agency," *Social Work Journal*, XXX, No. 2 (April, 1949), p. 87.

CHAPTER VII

A PROPOSAL FOR
AN INSTITUTE FOR RESEARCH
IN SOCIAL WORK

MICHIGAN has three professional schools of social work which are part of the three large universities in the state. Any one, or all three, of these schools is a potential location for an institute of the type recommended in this report. It seems improbable that all three schools will want to launch simultaneously into a program as experimental as the one proposed. It would probably be unfortunate if they did. There are other approaches to the task of improving and extending research in social work which have not been developed in detail in this report and which may fit the resources and the present programs of some of the schools of social work in Michigan better than can a research institute. An institute has been suggested as providing the best approach to overcoming some of the obstacles that in the past have hindered research in social work, but it would be unfortunate if the impression were left that the choice is between an institute or nothing. Each pattern for conducting research noted in the preceding chapter has its own special merits and may fit the resources and interests of particular universities or agencies better than an institute.

In considering the way to move from reconnaissance into action, the first essential if the proposal for an institute is to have any chance of realization is that the university and the school of social work launching the institute understand it and be thoroughly committed to it. The shift in orientation to the whole field of social work (its body of knowledge, its institutional forms, its practice) which occurs when an attempt is made to integrate social work theory and practice with the approaches and the concepts of social science—this shift in orientation will have its effect on the whole educational program of the school. Indeed, if this does not happen, the institute will have failed. Therefore a school of social work launching the kind of institute proposed really has to "be on fire about the idea," to use the phrase of one of the consultants to the Reconnaissance Study.

Secondly, there has to be from the outset a recognition that the institute, while starting with a director and possibly an associate, will have to move within a reasonable period to a staff of several persons if its objectives are to be realized. Unless this development is definitely in prospect there is little possibility that the kind of personnel or financial support required for a major departure in social work research can be attracted.

Assuming there is readiness to move toward establishment of an institute for research in social work, the two practical tasks to be dealt with are obtaining financial support and personnel. The difficulty here is that personnel cannot be obtained until there are finances, and finances are difficult to attract until the personnel is known. At one point in the Reconnaissance Study a foundation executive who has supervised the granting of several million dollars for research was asked how to "move off dead center" in this situation. This is what he said:

The first thing to do is to show that there is serious intent to do something of the kind you are proposing. A school can't sit back and say if we get some money we'll start thinking and looking at people. It has to say, "Look, we need such and such a type of man or men to do this job. We have reason to believe that Smith or

Jones would be interested in coming with it if there were adequate support for it in sight. We can carry this much of the load (it may not be very much) and we need so much money." This is the process.

There are different kinds of money available. Some foundations won't touch a project unless it has been worked out in detail. Others like to go in on the developmental side. Naturally you will go to foundations of the latter type.

Since some idea of personnel requirements would be needed before exploration of sources for financial support could go very far, we will consider the problem of personnel first.

PERSONNEL

In discussing personnel, a word must be said first as to the pace at which an institute might be expected to develop, since some notions about timing are required in order to make possible a plan for recruitment of personnel and development of a budget. Experts in child development have reported that the important thing in the growth of a child is not so much the level of achievement he may have realized at any particular chronological age, but the appearance in the proper combination and sequence of appropriate skills and attributes. In a new enterprise like a research institute, the rate of growth is not so crucial as the successful completion of the various stages in getting under way. We mention specific periods of time in the following discussion in order to give the discussion concreteness and to provide some basis for budget estimates, but the pace at which an institute might develop would depend on a variety of circumstances.

The first step in getting an institute staffed would be the selection of a director. The director must be able to plan the development of a research program in the uncharted area between social science and social work. He must be able to attract the kind of personnel who can do research in this area and weld them into a team. He must be able to do a "selling job" on his program to win acceptance and cooperation for it from professional social workers and from agencies and to develop the basis for continuing financial support. And he has to understand administration both for purposes of internal direction of the institute and for purposes of working out a sound pattern of relationships within the school of social work and with other departments and units of the university.

Ideally, the director should have both a scientific and professional background. The individual with this kind of training, plus the more intangible but just as important selling and administrative abilities, is extremely rare. A more realistic goal would probably be to seek a person with the leadership abilities mentioned and an understanding of and commitment to the task of bridging the gap between social work and the social sciences, and then to plan on supplementing him through an associate with particular strength in either social work or social science. This is admittedly a compromise. The long-range solution to the problem of staffing research enterprises in social work lies in the direction of training a certain number of persons who know the field of social work and are identified with it professionally, and who also are equipped as social scientists. To recognize the need for some persons who are so trained is not to say that everyone undertaking research in social work has to be equally well qualified in both social science and social work in order to make a contribution.

Once a director of the institute has been selected, an associate to work with him should be added as soon as the director is able to decide what kind of person he wants and is able to recruit him. The early addition of an associate is important, not simply because of the special knowledge he may contribute during the planning and developmental stage, but because the interaction of two minds working on a problem is apt to produce a better and quicker result than one mind working alone. This is particularly true where cross-disciplinary work is called for.

The addition of other staff to the institute should be gradual in order that new members may be absorbed and new additions may be made to complement existing staff. By the beginning of the second year the program of the institute may have been defined sufficiently that the specific qualifications of some of the additional staff members will have emerged. By the end of the third year it might be hoped that the institute could be staffed with five or six research persons.

The primary task in the initial stage of the institute's development would be one of planning. During this period also the basis should be laid for a solid integration of the research institute into the school of social work and for building cooperative working relationships with the social science departments in the university and with agencies in the state. An institute of the type proposed being so new, time should be allowed for the director to get acquainted with similar institutes functioning in other professional fields and for him to formulate principles and policies for the institute and to test these out in conference with others.

Before personnel recruitment could go very far, the particular areas of social work activity in which the major research of the institute would be done would have to be selected. Group work, community organization, child welfare, and public assistance—to name a few areas of social work practice—present quite different types of research problems, and a research institute could not be expected to operate with equal facility in relation to all of them. It would seem logical for the institute to select the areas of social work practice for research to which the school was devoting a substantial portion of its training facilities.

During the initial stage in the institute's development one or two specific projects of a limited nature should be carried out in which the goal would be to produce specific findings of immediate significance to the field of social work practice and administration. Stress has been placed previously in this report on the need for long-range programming of research in social work, and this is fundamental. But the ability of the institute to attract money and to develop cooperative arrangements for research with agencies will be furthered by a demonstration that researchers are practical people with something useful to say about social work practice and administration. Provision for this type of activity will also furnish both a stimulus and a corrective to work going forward on the long-range planning of the program of the institute.

To keep such projects from making too heavy inroads on the time of the staff during the initial period, they might well be worked out on a cooperative basis with a social science department or research organization of the university. This would have the advantage of providing some experience in collaborative work and would eliminate the need for adding staff to the institute before its long-range program was formulated. Money should be available to finance *ad hoc* staff from other departments for such purposes.

The personnel budget.—The number of positions to be established and the salaries to be attached to these positions are matters which do not properly fall within the scope of this report, since they would depend upon the finances available, the policy of the university and the school of social work, and the plan for development of the institute as worked out by its director. Some notion of budget requirements for research staff is needed, however, in order to make possible consideration of the financial requirements of an institute.

The position levels and salary ranges in effect in one social science research organization of national reputation are presented here as source data for development of estimates on the cost of staffing an institute.

Position	Salary Range [a]
Executive Director	Not given
Program Director	$8,800–$11,000
Assistant Program Director	7,000– 8,500
Study Director	5,000– 7,000
Assistant Study Director	3,500– 5,000

[a] As of April, 1951.

The positions of Assistant Program Director and those above require the Doctor of Philosophy degree; the other positions assume various stages of progress in work on the doctorate.

If effective interdisciplinary collaboration is to be realized in an institute for research in social work, there must be represented in the institute knowledge and research experience both in social work and in the relevant social sciences. Three or four senior staff positions seem to be the minimum requirement in order to achieve this. Obviously, even this many senior positions could not provide for all the kinds of competence that would be desirable in a research staff, but it is assumed that the personnel resources of the institute would be greatly broadened through its location in a school of social work and through cooperative arrangements worked out with the social science departments in the university.

Using the medians of the salary ranges shown above as a general guide, a budget for the professional staff of an institute for research with a total of ten members might be as shown below. The academic rank which corresponds most closely with the positions listed is shown in parentheses after each position title.

Positions	Estimated Cost
1 Executive Director	$12,000
1 Associate Director (Professor)	10,000
2 Senior Research Specialists (Associate Professor) @ $8,000	16,000
2 Junior Research Specialists (Assistant Professor) @ $6,000	12,000
4 Research Assistants (Teaching Fellow) @ $4,000	16,000
Total	$66,000

It will be noted that the amount of money proposed for investment in the higher positions is large in relation to the amount of money for the lower positions, which are essentially training positions. The training function of the institute would not be ready to operate until its program were fairly well established. Meanwhile, the planning and developmental work and the conduct of initial projects would require persons of high caliber. This does not mean necessarily persons who have already achieved eminence in their fields, but persons whose capacity to contribute has been demonstrated.

A five-year budget estimate.—The overhead and operating costs of an institute of research in social work are difficult to estimate since they would depend on the type of projects undertaken. Some projects require little more than a desk and a typewriter, while others require statistical clerks, tabulating machines, field interviewers, etc. To get some basis for estimates on overhead, the costs of operation for projects conducted by the Institute for Social Research at the University of Michigan were reviewed, and the various items figured as percentages of the personnel budget. Using a personnel budget of $66,000, the following additional costs in operating an institute are estimated:

Item	Cost
Annuities	$ 2,640
Clerical services	22,000
Equipment	3,500
Travel	6,600
Coding and tabulating	4,620
Communications and postage	1,980
Mimeographing	990
Total	$42,330

The total of the above items is approximately two-thirds of the proposed personnel budget. In calculating the total budget for an institute of research in social work it would therefore seem justifiable to add to the personnel item an amount for overhead and operations of two-thirds the amount estimated for personnel. This procedure has been followed in developing an estimate of the cost of operating an institute for the first five years.

After an institute had been launched it would take three or four years to bring it up to the size proposed in this report; for this reason a five-year budget is shown, broken down by year to indicate the gradual increase in staff that is envisaged. Costs for housing the institute are not included.

Table 5. Suggested Five-Year Budget for Institute of Research in Social Work

First Year	
Executive Director	$12,000
Associate Director (half year)	5,000
Special personnel from other departments	5,000
Overhead and operations costs (two-thirds of above)	14,700
	$ 36,700

Table 5. Suggested Five-Year Budget for Institute of Research in Social Work (Continued)

Second Year		
Executive Director	$12,000	
Associate Director	10,000	
Senior Research Specialist (half year)	4,000	
Junior Research Specialist (half year)	3,000	
Special personnel from other departments	2,500	
Overhead and operations costs (two-thirds of above)	21,000	
		$52,500
Third Year		
Executive Director	12,000	
Associate Director	10,000	
Senior Research Specialist	8,000	
Junior Research Specialist	6,000	
Two Research Assistants @ $4,000	8,000	
Overhead and operations costs (two-thirds of above)	29,300	
		73,300
Fourth Year		
Executive Director	12,000	
Associate Director	10,000	
Two Senior Research Specialists @ $8,000	16,000	
Two Junior Research Specialists @ $6,000	12,000	
Four Research Assistants @ $4,000	16,000	
Overhead and operations costs (two-thirds of above)	44,000	
		110,000
Fifth Year		
Same as Fourth Year		110,000
Total for five years		$382,500

Arbitrary as such a five-year budget estimate is, it provides a basis for consideration of the kind of financing an institute might require. Probably an amount between $350,000 and $400,000, exclusive of housing, for the first five years of operation represents a reasonable figure, with perhaps one-fourth of this available for the first two years and the balance for the remaining three years.

FINANCING

There are four sources of funds for the kind of institute proposed: the university, private individuals or foundations, government, and voluntary social agencies.

Universities.—It is assumed that the university launching a substantial research program in social work will be willing to apply university research funds to the program. Such funds for social science research are not extensive in most universities, and the demand on them is heavy. While it is not probable that a sizeable proportion of the suggested budget for an institute could be met out of regular university funds, universities frequently are able to contribute space and equipment to house research financed primarily with outside funds.

Foundations and individuals.—Private foundations or individuals should probably be expected to carry major responsibility for financing the institute over the first five-year period. Emerson Andrews has stated in his book, *Philanthropic Giving*, "Foundations are the 'venture capital' of philanthropy. . . . Because of [their] position of unusual freedom, they have an opportunity, and perhaps a special responsibility, for helping push forward today's most important frontier—the study of man himself and his relationships." [1] A project such as the

[1] Emerson Andrews, *Philanthropic Giving* (New York: Russell Sage Foundation, 1951), p. 103.

institute described calls for the investment of venture capital. It will take time for any research venture of the kind proposed to become established, develop a program, recruit a staff, and build up a reputation that will enable it to attract funds from operating programs for research in social work. During this period, particularly, funds are needed which are given on an unrestricted basis, rather than for support of work on particular problems. Foundations are the most appropriate source for such funds. Once established and staffed with an interdisciplinary team of scientists, it should be possible to obtain a substantial portion of funds for a continuing program from the budgets of social work programs. There will always be the need, however, for foundation grants to support long-range developmental work and for the support of researchers in training.

Government.—Governmental support of research in various scientific fields has expanded tremendously in recent years. Two types of financial support have been given: grants-in-aid and research contracts. The President's Scientific Research Board in its report to the President on the nation's medical research in 1947 put the distinction between these two types of support as follows:

A grant-in-aid for medical research is made for the support of a project suggested by an investigator out of his own curiosity and interest. The emphasis is upon aiding a scientist likely to make a contribution to existing knowledge. The immediate subject of the project, the broader problem of which it forms a part, and the scientific field to which it belongs are of relatively little concern to the grantor. . . .

The research contract is used by industry, the Army, and the Veterans' Administration to purchase the services of an investigator to work on a defined problem. . . . Generally, the contract is a device whereby industry and certain Government agencies purchase research and research services which they need but do not have.[2]

The National Institute of Mental Health of the U.S. Public Health Service is the only governmental organization with a program of research grants-in-aid for work on problems which fall within the field of social work. The program of the institute is focused on the causes, diagnosis, treatment, control, and prevention of mental diseases, and since a number of social work programs, particularly those employing psychiatric social workers, are concerned with these problems some financial support from this source might be expected.

Of the ninety projects receiving support from the Institute of Mental Health as of January 1, 1951, only four were focused on problems of specific concern to social work, although a great many more were concerned with basic research on problems of general significance to social work and other fields. Of the four, one dealt with marital counseling, two with institutional or group treatment of disturbed children, and one with coordination of community mental health leadership. The major reason for the smaller number of grants in the area of social work, according to the staff of the institute, is that very few projects have been submitted, and most of these did not meet the standards set up by the National Advisory Mental Health Council.

While the annual grants of the National Institute of Mental Health are not large, a grant from this source could support at least one senior investigator and, depending on the needs of the project, could be renewed over a three- or four-year period. Because such grants are authorized for individual investigators

[2] John R. Steelman, *The Nation's Medical Research,* Vol. V of *Science and Public Policy.* A report to the President by the Chairman of the President's Scientific Research Board (Washington, D.C.: Government Printing Office, 1947), p. 60.

to work on particular problems and are not available for support of a general research budget, they must always be regarded as supplemental to an ongoing program.

Research contracts have not been used extensively by governmental welfare agencies to finance research, although such programs usually have authority to purchase services of various kinds on a contract basis. The Children's Bureau of the Federal Security Agency included for the first time in 1951 a statement in its policy manual which specifically authorized the expenditure of federal child welfare services funds for contract research. The manual states that federal child welfare services funds may be used for "purchase for a special research project or for consultation on research in the child welfare program of services of (a) a public or voluntary organization, such as a foundation or university; (b) a research worker or consultant." [3] Since child welfare services funds are spent only through state child welfare programs, the state program must initiate the plan to use child welfare funds for contract research.

Public assistance is the program in which the most money is being spent. While more money for research is going into this program than into any other social work program in Michigan, the research is entirely operational or administrative in character. Mr. Willis Oosterhof, Director of Research and Statistics in the State Department of Social Welfare, has pointed out problems needing analysis in the program which go beyond the resources of his division and which might well be undertaken by a university-related research center. Many of these problems call for specialized personnel which cannot appropriately be added to the regular research staff of the Department. Over a period of time it should be possible to work out cooperative arrangements with this Department which would

---

[3] U.S. Children's Bureau, Federal Security Agency, Washington, D.C. *Policy Manual for the Use of Federal Child Welfare Services Funds* (April, 1951).

permit a substantial amount of financial support to go to a research institute for work on problems in the area of public assistance.

There are other welfare programs, such as the state training schools for juvenile delinquents and rehabilitative services for the blind, where substantial amounts of money are being spent each year with little systematic research on the effectiveness of various policies and procedures. The availability of a resource such as the proposed institute would make possible the conduct of research on these programs which now goes undone, not so much for lack of money as for lack of an awareness of the potential contribution of research and of an effective way of using money for research.

Voluntary social work.—One of the most important contributions which voluntary social work agencies have made is the development and testing-out of new methods of meeting needs in our society. This role of the voluntary agencies is still one of the most important reasons for their continuance and support. Implied in this role is research by which the results of services can be appraised, yet few voluntary agencies are equipped to conduct such research.

What research is done at present in the voluntary field is conducted for the most part by community chests and councils as an adjunct to their planning and budgeting operations. The Detroit Council of Social Agencies, for instance, spent $24,000 for its research program in 1950. From time to time agencies or councils of social agencies will have a special survey done by a national organization or an individual consultant. These surveys, while of limited value as research undertakings, indicate the readiness of private agencies to invest money in studies to improve their services.

One of the factors which has hindered the small private agency from doing research on its activities is the fact that it is too small to support a research staff of its own, and the material available in its own case load may be too limited to permit productive research. One way of circumventing this problem is to pool the resources of several small agencies for a piece of research. This can be done either through direct appropriation of funds by the central fund-raising agency, or by special arrangement between a group of agencies operating in the same field. Such a development is not likely to come about without some stimulation and without a resource available to which an agency might turn for research, such as an institute for research in social work.

Over $15 million was spent by community chest agencies in Michigan during 1950 and an additional $550 thousand was spent by American Red Cross Home Service. This sum was divided among over 300 agencies in local communities. It would be a sizeable task to develop the arrangements whereby agencies could pool their resources for the support of research on special problems. Nevertheless, the interest among agencies in an expanded use of research in their programs should provide encouragement for undertaking this task. The fact that this Reconnaissance Study has been sponsored by the Michigan Welfare League, which is a kind of state-wide council of social agencies, is one bit of evidence of the readiness of agencies and organizations in social work to meet more adequately their responsibilities for research.

Philip Klein's suggestion at the 1948 National Conference of Social Work that agencies set aside 2 percent of their operating budgets for research is worthy of careful consideration. The percentage figure suggested is not the important element in the proposal, but rather the principle behind it. Although a large amount of money from agencies probably could not be anticipated while the institute was being established, the investment by voluntary agencies of some funds in an institute during its early stages would strengthen it out of all proportion to the amount of money involved. Agencies would feel a more vital relationship to a project into which they were putting money and would be more apt to study the application of research undertaken by the institute to their own agencies.

Before a long-range plan can be developed for tapping funds in voluntary social work agencies for support of a research program, the institutional arrangements have to be set up toward which financial support can be directed. It is a rather dubious service to agencies at present to arouse their interest in undertaking research in relation to their programs without providing some concrete suggestions as to how their interest can be given effective expression. Establishment of an institute would provide a facility to which agencies could turn when they want research done. Until some such facility is available which is adequately equipped in terms of personnel and organization the large potential in the private agency field for support of research cannot be tapped.

CONCLUSION

One final word should be said on the launching of an institute for research in social work. There comes a point in discussing the needs and potentialities of research in social work when further progress can be made only through getting some research under way and learning through doing. It is possible in a reconnoitering operation to get the general lay of the land, identify the obstacles, and pick out the points where an attack appears most likely to succeed. But the best-laid plans may be disproved by the first encounter. Reliance must be placed on those carrying forward the proposals in this study to observe and learn and modify their approach as they go along.

No plan will succeed unless it is pursued with determination and vigor. The proposal for an institute for research in social work, located in a professional school of social work in a university and staffed with an interdisciplinary team of social scientists and social workers, has the merit, at least, of being a different approach than any tried up to this time in social work. Even if it should prove wrong, the experience of attempting it should move the field of social work nearer to an effective use of research in discharging its responsibilities to individuals and to the community.

PROBLEMS IN SOCIAL WORK PRACTICE, ORGANIZATION, AND KNOWLEDGE NEEDING EVALUATIVE RESEARCH

THE PROCEDURE FOR IDENTIFYING PROBLEMS

THREE CONFERENCES were held during the Reconnaissance Study to identify specific problems which, from the standpoint of operating programs, call for evaluative research. One conference was focused on problems in the field of child welfare, a second on problems in the family service field, and a third on problems in the field of public assistance. Other fields such as medical social work, probation and parole, and group work were not explored due to lack of time.

The conferences were attended by practitioners, agency administrators, community organization specialists, social work educators, representatives of related professions, and agency board members. Participants were asked to make their questions evaluative in character, although in the conferences many other types of questions were raised and some of these are reported here. Participants were also told not to attempt to phrase or limit their questions in such a way as to make them amenable to research. The purpose of the conferences was not to outline a number of specific research projects, but to provide research workers in social work and in the social sciences a listing of problems which, from the standpoint of operating social work programs, need study. Some of the questions raised, it will be noted, do not lend themselves to research at all, but fall in the field of values and ethics. The ques-

tions have been grouped under six headings for presentation here:
Questions about the goals of social work programs
Questions about the practical outcome of social work programs, practices, and policies
Questions about the assumptions and theories on which policy and practice rest
Questions about the effect of community attitudes and understanding on the effectiveness of social work services
Questions about the influence of cultural, economic, and other forces on the outcome of services
Questions about the effect of social work practices and policies on attitudes and values in the community

Under the third grouping of questions, those relating to assumptions and theories, there has been included a listing prepared by a faculty committee of the New York School of Social Work.

The names of the participants in the conferences are listed at the end of this appendix.

QUESTIONS ABOUT THE GOALS OF SOCIAL WORK PROGRAMS

How adequate is the community's understanding of the function of the family service agency as stated by staff and board, and to the extent that it understands the function, does it approve it?

Does the staff and board members' conception of the needs in the community to which the family agency should direct its efforts correspond with the felt need in the community for service from the family agency?

Are our methods of interpreting assistance policies to the public able to elicit the same attitudes toward *classes* of individuals as those the public may have toward individual cases?

What differences exist between various groups in the population with respect to the goals of any particular service? For instance, would divorce be regarded by all groups in the population as a successful conclusion to some of the situations brought to a marriage counseling service?

Is there a significant difference between the caseworkers' criteria of success in a family agency and the criteria used by members of the community, and if so, what effect has this difference on the ability of the agency to serve the community?

To what extent have policies in administering public assistance kept up with changing attitudes and values in our culture, as reflected in the passage of the social security act, the emergence of the Townsend and similar movements, the development of pension plans in industry, etc.?

Is inducing a particular behavior pattern (in contrast to resolving a child's emotional conflicts) an effective way of realizing one of the goals of a correctional institution, which is to return the child to society in such a condition that he will not continue to violate society's rules?

Have the virtual cessation of the relief-giving function in family service agencies and the focus of attention on problems within the individual which hinder his functioning in society resulted in the failure of the family agency to recognize and deal with some of the more simple and manageable problems which may come to it, such as problems of financial management, knowledge and use of community resources, etc.?

Are our public assistance policies and casework techniques geared to short-term dependency, with periodic reestablishment of eligibility for assistance, so that the problem of long-term chronic dependency cannot be attacked?

QUESTIONS ABOUT THE PRACTICAL OUTCOME OF SOCIAL
WORK PROGRAMS, PRACTICES, AND POLICIES

How successful are adoptions, in terms of both parents and child, where the adoptive parents are over forty years of age?

How do adoptive placements made through well established and well staffed agencies compare, in terms of the adjustment of the child to his adoptive parents, with placements arranged through private individuals such as doctor and lawyers?

What is the effect on children of placement in a number of different boarding homes? Is their sense of identity, of who they are and where they belong in the world, affected in a way that is not true for children with a stable boarding-home placement?

What are the effects of group care for children under two years of age, as compared with foster care in private homes of the kind available to agencies with young children?

How adequate are boarding-home placements arranged by parents as compared with boarding-home placements made through agencies and supervised by them? [The extensive development of so-called independent boarding homes in Michigan and the attempts of the state to protect children in these homes through a licensing procedure gave rise to this question.—EDITOR.]

What is the cost and effectiveness of homemaker service as a substitute for foster care in certain relatively short-term cases?

What is the effect, in terms of modifying behavior, of a policy in a boys' training school which removes from the hands of cottage parents the administration of disciplinary measures and puts it in the hands of a cottage-life supervisor? Does the distance thus created between the commission of an act and the consequences of that act reduce significantly the learning value of the discipline? What is the effect of this policy on the role of the cottage parent as a substitute parent to the boy in the institution? [A correlated question raised was whether, given the kind of cottage parents frequently found in a public correctional school, some means other than such a rigid rule was available for protecting boys in the institution from physical brutality.—EDITOR.]

Are authoritative agencies, such as the courts, better able to treat certain kinds of situations than the nonauthoritative, and what are these situations?

Is a child easier to deal with if he has been routed through the official legal orbit and then returned to the same community and same classroom than if the judicial agency had not been used?

What is the optimum size unit for different types of social work programs—a child guidance clinic, foster home placement agency, family service agency, probation department, institution for delinquent children?

Does the present method of identifying the problems of persons coming to family agencies make it possible to give priority to those problems where immediate attention is important in preventing further damage?

Does the practice of recording a diagnosis and treatment plan in a case increase significantly the clarity of the worker with respect to the problem presented and the goals of treatment?

Are interviews that cost $15.00 under a particular system which provides for detailed recording and supervision sufficiently superior to interviews which cost half this much, but do not provide for recording and supervision, that the added investment is justified?

How effective is the present generally used method of recording in family service agencies, in terms of facilitating service to clients, as compared with the method used in psychiatry of recording immediately after each interview a brief note on the case?

Is it more effective to use the number of limited mental hygiene personnel for treatment of individual children, or to use them for staff education with other professional personnel such as teachers, court officials, etc.? Under what circumstances is a combination of direct and indirect service most effective?

Is the freedom to finance rehabilitative measures which the Red Cross has in working with disaster victims more economical in the long run than the restrictive measures available to the public assistance agency? For instance, a little spending over a long period will keep a recipient alive, but not much else, whereas the same amount of spending concentrated in a short period and focused on the problem which is causing the dependency might restore the person to self-support.

What is the effect of an agency policy which makes it necessary for a worker to withdraw from a case the minute, as a result of rehabilitative efforts, the client begins to be self-supporting? Is this the time to terminate assistance and service?

What is the effect of having the assistance grant approximately equal to the income level of other members of the community, in contrast to having the assistance grant at a considerably lower level than the income of other members of the community? [It was noted that such a study could be made in counties of two states which were economically and socially comparable, but where the relief policies differed in this way.—EDITOR.]

What is the effect on aged people of having to liquidate their property or give a lien to the state in order to obtain assistance?

What is the effect on older people of their children being compelled to contribute to their support in order for them to be eligible for old-age assistance?

What is the effect of grants under the old age and survivors insurance program as compared with the old age assistance program in terms of strengthening the individual's desires and capacity to be self-directing?

Is public assistance less expensive, in terms of long-range costs, when the caseworker is guided by very broad rules or when the caseworker operates to the letter of a very strict law?

What has been the effect of federated fund-raising on community understanding of and support for various social work programs? What is the effect of automatic deductions from pay checks for community fund contributions on understanding of agency programs?

What is the effect of different methods of rejecting applicants for adoptive children on the community's understanding of and support for sound adoptive practices?

Have state and federal matching funds in various public social work programs had the effect of increasing the community's sense of responsibility for these programs, or has it had the effect of lessening that sense of responsibility?

Is chronological order of application a sufficient criterion for acceptance for service?

What happens to families which are rejected because of lack of residence? How many accept referral back to their place of residence, how many stay on in the community and work out something else, and how satisfactory is the alternative arrangement?

Is there evidence that persons now on relief who were children of families on relief during the '30's are now financially dependent because of the effects, among other things, of their earlier relief experience?

What is the effect in disability cases of the requirement of total disability in terms of fostering continued dependency by recipients?

Has it been a good arrangement to have rehabilitation for the blind administered by the same persons who are carrying cases of financial assistance for the blind?

What happens to the attitudes and personalities of people who have
been on relief for a long period of time?

What is the effect of unearned income on initiative and productiv-
ity, both in the assistance programs and in the unemployment
insurance programs?

To what extent do "self-referred" clients tend to come from the
more intellectual strata of society where there is an ability to
verbalize problems, and to what extent does this method of
bringing clients to the agency tend to cut out certain other
strata in society?

What happens to people who apply to agencies for service and are
rejected either because the agency has no more facilities or because the service requested is not one that the agency provides?
[A study might be conducted on the effect of rejection on the
further use of community facilities, and on the way the rejected
applicant handled the problem which brought about the referral.—EDITOR.]

One of the objectives of the federally supported county child welfare service programs in Michigan has been not simply to provide
service to children, but also to raise the level of community understanding and use of resources for children. Have the programs had the effect of making communities more intelligent
about the needs of children and the kinds of services available
for them?

How effective are single interview cases, which constitute a fairly
large proportion of cases coming to the family service agency, in
assisting the individual to identify and deal with the problem
which brought him to the agency? How many such cases turn
up at another point in the community with a problem which
might have been identified and dealt with at the family service
agency?

How many single interview cases are terminated at the initiative of
the agency, and how many are terminated because of the failure
of the client to come back a second time?

What proportion of the problems brought to family service agencies are ones which can characteristically be disposed of in one
interview?

What is the effect of brief mental hygiene educational programs on parents in enabling them to deal more understandingly and effectively with their children? Does the insecurity and guilt aroused in some parents make them less able to cope effectively with problems in child-rearing?

What has happened to the children of families who were on relief five, ten, and fifteen years ago?

How does the adjustment of children in families where the mother took employment during the war and left the assistance rolls compare with the adjustment of children in families where the mother remained on assistance and continued to care for her children herself?

What is the effectiveness of a children's agency staffed by trained social workers, as compared with an agency which does not employ trained workers?

How effective are present methods of screening workers for social service positions, both in the schools, in civil service, and in agencies?

How valid is the use of volunteers in a family casework program? Can the concept of the nurse's aid be introduced into a family agency?

How does the relatively short period of time which many case-workers spend in a particular job affect the service being provided by these workers?

What is the cost of a high rate of staff turnover in terms of need for staff training, closer supervision, lessened efficiency in handling cases, learning of agency policies and community resources, etc.?

What are the causal factors in personnel turnover, what is needed to eliminate those causal factors, and how far is the public willing to go in supporting measures which will eliminate them?

What are the kinds of skills required to do a rehabilitative job with public assistance clients, and is it realistic to talk about having these skills represented in the quantity needed in the public assistance programs in Michigan, given present salary levels and training facilities?

What are the services provided by the public assistance worker? What do these services do to meet the problem of the public assistance client? How do these services relate to the basic purposes of public assistance?

What is an optimum case load for a worker in a family service agency? What is the number of casework interviews which may be expected from a caseworker in the course of a month?

Is the use of caseworkers in committees or in family life education programs an efficient use of their skills and training?

What is the most effective size for an administrative unit in the public welfare field? If Detroit could do what it wanted to, would it set up five or seven or ten administrative units instead of trying to administer all its programs through three big offices?

Is there an increase in the effectiveness of the following programs when they are integrated into a single county welfare department, instead of operating as separate units within the county: categorical financial assistance, general assistance, child welfare, rehabilitative services for the blind?

Should a child welfare worker be attached to a county welfare department or a juvenile court?

How effective in relation to cost are such devices as the operating manual, casework supervision, staff meetings, etc., in keeping staff informed of resources in the agency and in the larger community?

How effective is the present structure for providing clearance and coordination of service among agencies so that each agency may know what services can be expected from all the other agencies, thus avoiding misreferral of persons seeking help?

From the standpoint of the individual needing help, how understandable and usable is the present structure of social services which locates substantially similar activities in three or four agencies, such as the family service agency, the visiting teacher service, and the child guidance clinic?

What is the effect of "buck-passing" between agencies on community understanding and support of agency services?

When is it desirable to set up a new agency or a separate unit of an existing agency to administer a new service, and when is it desirable to integrate it into an existing agency or unit?

How do you effectively coordinate the state employment service and the federally supported vocational rehabilitation program in Michigan with the public assistance programs, taking into account the separate governmental levels and the separate agency structures? What are the most effective devices for obtaining cooperative planning and service?

How desirable is the administrative structure which lodges protective responsibility for children in one agency and placement responsibility in another agency?

QUESTIONS ABOUT THE ASSUMPTIONS AND THEORIES ON WHICH POLICY AND PRACTICE REST

We hear frequent reference to the "real" problem in a particular case. To what extent is the perception of the "real" problem determined by the philosophical orientation of the worker or the school of social work from which the worker may have graduated? There seems to be a tendency to classify persons in terms of personality structure, for instance, and to pay little attention to socio-economic and cultural factors.

To what extent have the concepts used by psychiatrically oriented social workers in understanding and dealing with children been validated, so that they may be properly described as "knowledge"?

What is the validity of the theory that delinquent behavior in a child represents an inner need on the part of the child for counter-aggression?

How well established is our knowledge of an infant's needs for mothering at different ages? A psychiatrist stated that he regarded as established knowledge the statement that infants need mothers and that psychopathic personalities may develop as a result of the lack of mothering during the first two years. A child welfare administrator challenged the assertion that this was knowledge, and declared that if it were, the state would be in a position to close down certain children's institutions presently operating in Michigan.

What is the validity of a number of basic assumptions now made regarding the psychological import to the recipient of asking for and receiving aid within the public welfare setting, and how adequately is this knowledge being applied by individual workers in current public assistance programs?

What is the optimum age for adoption in light of all the factors that have to be considered? We have seen in recent years a lowering of the age for placing children for adoption. It used to be considered dangerous to place a child before the age of one year. We now find agencies placing a child at the age of ten days, three months, or some other arbitrary figure.

How adequate are the criteria for selecting persons on public assistance for rehabilitative work? Would less attention to the exceedingly difficult case and more to the marginal case produce greater results?

The following list of assumptions, concepts, and theories which require testing was prepared by a faculty committee of the New York School of Social Work.[1]

Personality growth requires the meeting of certain basic needs (physical, intellectual, social, or relationship).

Beyond a certain point the gratification of needs promotes dependency (so that an overprotected child does not mature, a relief recipient given a satisfying allowance does not work, etc.).

There is therapeutic value in promoting expression of feeling (catharsis).

Immediate family members are ordinarily the key figures for identification and sources of values for the growing child.

The adult leader is an important component in a children's group in a settlement or center.

Groups of children of adolescent age should be encouraged to affiliate with centers and settlements rather than function independently without affiliation.

Growth of individuals in a club and of the club as such are best promoted when the leader is an "enabler" rather than a person with a program.

In community organization the proper process of gaining partici-

---

[1] Unpublished draft of memorandum entitled "Prospectus for a Proposed Research Center at the New York School of Social Work, Columbia University." Prepared by a faculty committee composed of Philip Klein, Alfred Kahn, and Sophia Robison. April, 1950. Pp. 13–14.

pation is more important (from a long-range point of view) than the specific immediate achievements.

Social work practitioners in casework, group work, and community organization better serve their clientele when trained in personality dynamics to understand the latent, as well as manifest, meaning of behavior.

Certain kinds of understanding and skill are best achieved through social work training, in contrast to the understanding and skills which derive from psychiatric and psychological training.

From the point of view of parent and/or child, certain social work settings (court, school clinic) have more "authority" to require participation than do others (welfare agencies, guidance clinics, settlements).

Government welfare programs must be more impersonal, and less capable of individualization, than voluntary programs.

Casework procedure based on a "diagnostic approach" more nearly meets the needs of most adults and children than do procedures based on other theories (Rankian, Rogerian, etc.).

QUESTIONS ABOUT THE EFFECT OF COMMUNITY ATTITUDES
AND UNDERSTANDING ON THE EFFECTIVENESS OF SOCIAL
WORK SERVICES

What is the effect of the tradition of philanthropy, which is such a part of private social agencies, on the use of the resources of the agency by all members of the community?

What is the clients' evaluation of the services they have received from social work agencies, and is their evaluation of more significance than, say, that of the worker or board member?

Are the one-interview cases due to misreferrals?

What is the effect of different methods of rejecting applicants for adoptive children on the community's understanding of and support for sound adoptive practices?

How valid is the notion that persons can benefit from casework service in family agencies only if they come voluntarily? Certain cases of neglect are now being carried in one agency at the request of the juvenile court where the client does not come out of choice.

QUESTIONS ABOUT THE INFLUENCE OF CULTURAL,
ECONOMIC, AND OTHER SOCIAL FORCES ON THE
OUTCOME OF SERVICES

Is there a significant difference between urban and rural communities in respect to the effect of a physical handicap in making a man unemployable? What types of "protected" employment are available in a rural community?

To what extent does racial discrimination account for unemployment which results in dependence on public assistance?

What is the success of adoption, both in terms of the child and of the adoptive parents, in those cases where the child has known his own parents as compared with those where the child has not known his parents, holding the factor of age constant?

How adequate is our knowledge of differences in cultural backgrounds which may account for apparent differences in the success of an individual's adjustment? For instance, Allison Davis has pointed out that aggressive conduct and little respect for property may represent a successful adjustment of a child in one cultural group, where these same characteristics would represent failure in certain other cultural groups.

How account for the fact that one group of people will go on public assistance and another group, who are equally eligible under the law, will not?

What proportion of the unemployment found among relief recipients can be accounted for by the fact that the individual has not happened to be at the right gate at the right time?

What are the factors that influence foster parents to board children, and, particularly, what is the effect of boarding rates on ability to find adequate foster homes?

QUESTIONS ABOUT THE EFFECT OF SOCIAL WORK
PRACTICES AND POLICIES ON ATTITUDES AND VALUES
IN THE COMMUNITY

Is there any evidence that policies in the aid to dependent children program with respect to illegitimate children (that is, granting assistance on behalf of the child without regard for whether it is legitimate), actually have an effect on the extent of illegitimacy in our society?

What is the effect of present policies requiring that the older child in a family that is receiving aid to dependent children who is going out and making money at some job contribute all but a small portion of what he earns toward the support of the family? Is such a policy found to discourage the child from going out and seeking employment at a time when he should be developing attitudes of self-support and independence?

Would the elimination of legal responsibility of children to support their aged parents tend to support and encourage the general movement in our culture away from the moral responsibility of children for their parents?

Are cultural attitudes affected by administrative and legislative policies? In Louisiana, was the sense of responsibility of children for their aged parents diminished by establishment of an assistance program which was essentially of a pension character?

What is the effect of an arbitrary age limit of sixty-five in the social security program on the interest and ability of older people to continue an active and productive life?

What is the effect of our expanded social security program, including unemployment insurance, on the attitude of people toward work and on their sense of responsibility for providing for their own future?

PARTICIPANTS IN CONFERENCES
TO IDENTIFY PROBLEMS
FOR EVALUATIVE RESEARCH

Conference on Social Services for Children
May 3, 1951

Mrs. Elizabeth Armstrong, Children's Center of Metropolitan Detroit

Mrs. Mary Clark, D. A. Blodgett Home for Children, Grand Rapids

Dr. Gunnar Dybwad, Children's Division, Michigan State Department of Social Welfare, Lansing

Mrs. James Foster, James Foster Foundation, Ann Arbor

Miss Jean Godfrey, Michigan Children's Institute, Ann Arbor

Dr. Gilbert Krulee, Research Center for Group Dynamics, Ann Arbor

Mr. Frederick Lenhart, Catholic Service Bureau of Grand Rapids

Mr. David Prichard, Children's Division, Michigan State Department of Social Welfare, Kalamazoo

Dr. Ralph Rabinovitch, Neuropsychiatric Institute, University of Michigan, Ann Arbor

Mr. Clarence Ramsey, Michigan Children's Institute, Ann Arbor

Mrs. Josselyn Van Tyne, James Foster Foundation, Ann Arbor

Mrs. Maxine Virtue, James Foster Foundation Study of Services for Children in Michigan, Ann Arbor

Mr. Anthony Bratosich, Catholic Service Bureau of Muskegon

Mrs. Barbara Watt, Baptist Children's Home of Detroit

Conference on Family Service Agency Programs
June 6, 1951

Dr. Donald Bauma, Calvin College, Grand Rapids

Miss Winifred Bell, Adult Psychiatric Clinic, Harper's Hospital, Detroit

Mr. Charles B. Brink, School of Social Work, Wayne University, Detroit

Mr. Charles Brown, Family Service Society, Saginaw

Mrs. Eleanor Cranefield, School of Social Work, University of Michigan, Detroit

Mr. Edward Crowe, Catholic Youth Organization, Detroit

Rev. Sigmund Osmielowski, Catholic Charities, Detroit

Miss Evangeline Sheibley, Family and Child Welfare Division, Council of Social Agencies, Detroit

Mr. Harold Silver, Jewish Social Service Bureau, Detroit

Mr. Russell West, Board of Education, Ann Arbor

Conference on Public Assistance Programs
June 7, 1951

Mr. Harry Becker, United Auto Workers, Detroit

Miss Ruth Bowen, Michigan State Department of Social Welfare, Lansing

Mr. Thomas Cook, Michigan State Department of Social Welfare, Alpena

Miss Theresa Farrell, Council of Social Agencies, Flint

Mr. Fidele F. Fauri, School of Social Work, University of Michigan, Ann Arbor

Mrs. Blanche Funderburg, Michigan State Department of Social Welfare, Grand Rapids

Mr. John Hanks, Family Service Agency, Jackson

Mr. Michael Kreider, Michigan Welfare League, Lansing

Mr. Willis Oosterhof, Michigan State Department of Social Welfare, Lansing

Miss Helen Roninger, Bureau of Public Assistance, Federal Security Agency, Cleveland

Mrs. Mavis Townsend, Wayne County Bureau of Social Aid, Detroit

Rev. Joseph Walen, Catholic Service Bureau of Grand Rapids

Mr. Franklin Wallin, Michigan Welfare League, Jenison

Mrs. Patricia Rabinowitz, Bureau of Social Aid of Wayne County, Detroit

ANALYSES OF FOUR EVALUATIVE STUDIES IN SOCIAL WORK

PREPARED FOR THE
MICHIGAN RECONNAISSANCE STUDY BY
JOHN G. HILL, LEON FESTINGER,
HELEN L. WITMER, AND ALFRED J. KAHN

MEASURING RESULTS IN SOCIAL CASEWORK: A MANUAL ON JUDGING MOVEMENT, by J. McVicker Hunt and Leonard S. Kogan. New York: Family Service Association of America, 1950.

Analysis of Methodology by John G. Hill

The movement scale was developed under the auspices of the Community Service Society of New York in response to a directive from its board committee on the Institute of Welfare Research "to determine and express how casework is carried on, at what cost, and with what success." The study was originally begun in 1942 and the results of the work on the movement scale were published in two monographs by the Family Service Association of America in 1950.[1]

What the movement scale is and is not.—The movement scale is an attempt to measure casework results by standardizing and quantifying the judgment of casework practitioners on "the change that occurs in an individual client and/or his environment between the

[1] In addition to the Manual on Judging Movement, Hunt, Kogan, and Blenkner published a report on the use of the scale on a group of cases under the title *Testing Results in Social Casework: A Field-Test of the Movement Scale* (New York: Family Service Association of America, 1950).

opening and closing of his case." The decision to use the judgment of caseworkers, rather than some other feasible means of making the judgment, was due to several preliminary studies by the Institute of Welfare Research which led the authors of the movement scale to the conviction that the judgment of caseworkers is a "fairly reliable measuring tool." That is, the studies revealed a relatively high degree of agreement among workers independently judging the same cases when their judgments were based only on the definitions and standards acquired during the usual professional social work training. Also, use of the caseworker's judgment as the measuring instrument was considered to enhance the prospect that this method of evaluating casework might be adopted as routine procedure in agencies by making its application easier and less expensive than might be the case if possible alternative methods were employed.

The variable, and the only variable, which the movement scale is designed to measure is *movement*, defined as "the change that occurs in an individual client and/or his environment between opening and closing of his case." The movement scale, therefore, attempts to measure only the amount and direction of change in the client and/or his situation between two points in time, the opening and closing of his case or the opening of the case and some other point before it is closed when sufficient evidence has accumulated to enable the caseworker to judge whatever change may have occurred.

The movement concept was adopted to the exclusion of other factors in a complete evaluation of casework results and in preference to other possible approaches to the problem because of several considerations. First, the Institute of Welfare Research considered the change in the client and/or his situation to be the primary, though admittedly not the sole, question in evaluating the effectiveness of casework treatment. Second, the concept of movement is indigenous to casework and is universally understood and used by casework practitioners. Thus, its use would not inject a new and perhaps extraneous element into casework theory and practice which might prove to be a deterrent to its acceptance by the profession. Third, it provides a single though complex variable which cuts across the multiplicity of casework problems, precedures, services and results, thus simplifying what could be an inordinately complicated and costly procedure for routine application. Each additional factor besides movement required for a complete appraisal system would need an additional and perhaps more intricate scaling instrument. Fourth, since the movement concept relates only to the extent of change or the difference in adjustment of the client between the opening and closing of his case, it avoids the determination of absolute levels of personality or social adjustment. The measurement of absolute levels of adjustment would present exceedingly complicated problems, and there is some doubt whether any set of standards by which the absolute level of a person's social adjustment could be determined would gain wide and continued acceptance. Furthermore, in the words of the authors of the movement scale, "the concept of movement is an integral part of casework philosophy in that caseworkers aim to help their clients behave more happily and effectively—relative to their previous functioning—rather than to have them fit some idealistic pattern of static perfection."

The achievement of relative simplicity and possibly greater acceptance by the casework profession through exclusive use of the movement concept is not, however, without acknowledged loss. As already indicated, the movement score yields no information on the absolute status of the client's adjustment at the close of the case. It does not reveal at what level he is functioning in relation to his social milieu but only how his functioning at the close of casework treatment compares with that at the beginning of treatment. It provides no information on the nature of the client's problems or in what specific respects progress in their solution may have been made. It does not indicate the kinds of services he has been rendered nor does it evaluate services typically provided in casework, such as information on community resources, financial assistance, housekeeping service, vacations or camp, where such services are rendered without discernible evidence of change enduring longer than the services themselves. It does not encompass "brief service" cases, i.e., cases consisting of less than five interviews (currently comprising well over half of the case loads of family casework agencies), since the Institute's field test of the movement scale revealed that sufficient evidence of movement is usually not found in such cases.

By definition, it deliberately and explicitly excludes the degree to which casework treatment goals in a particular case were attained, the extent to which casework treatment may have prevented deterioration, and the degree of casework skill or extent of casework effort expended on a case. From the research point of view, the most serious limitation of the movement concept is that it takes no account of the extent to which casework treatment is or is not responsible for any movement of progress evident in a case.

In brief, therefore, the movement scale is a device for standardizing the judgment of caseworkers in answering this one simple and direct question: What progress, or deterioration, and how much occurred in the client and/or his situation between the time he began receiving casework service and the time that service was terminated, regardless of the cause of the change?

Establishing criteria against which success is to be measured.— The criteria for judging whether movement had taken place were developed empirically from the reasons given by a group of 15 caseworkers of the Family Service Department of the Community Service Society in rating the progress of 38 test cases. Examination and analysis of these reasons yielded four categories of criteria on which there was complete agreement. These were adopted as the basic criteria for judging movement. The four categories consist of changes in the client's—

1) Adaptive efficiency, such as his ability to get along with other people; efficiency on his job or in running a home; or overt changes in his competence in any other respect.
2) Disabling habits and conditions, such as changes in personality traits, basic emotional conflicts, and health.
3) Verbalized attitudes and understanding, such as accepting counsel; changes in attitudes toward himself or others shown by what he says; verbalized understanding of the relationship between his behavior and his attitudes or feelings.
4) Environmental circumstances, such as changes in living quarters, the behavior of other people toward the client, change resulting in child placement.

The criteria cited by some but not all or a majority of the caseworkers judging the test cases were also analyzed, grouped into categories, and explicitly eliminated as extraneous to the movement concept. The plan for formulating a scale to standardize judgments with an acceptable degree of reliability (i.e., agreement) required that discrepancies in judgment standards be held to a minimum. Since experimental work in judgment has demonstrated that agreement among independent judges is increased by allowing for the separate judgment of factors ruled to be extraneous to, but associated with, the principal judgment, the movement scale includes provision for separate scorings of these extraneous factors in order to prevent or reduce contamination of the movement ratings. There are eight such factors ruled out as not constituting criteria for judging movement: (1) Degree to which treatment goals were attained; (2) Degree to which casework is responsible for the movement evident in the case; (3) Degree of skill with which the case is managed; (4) Over-all amount of effort expended on the case; (5) Difficulty of the client's problem from the technical standpoint of successful casework treatment; (6) Movement might have occurred without casework but the rapidity of the movement was accelerated by casework; (7) Whether casework prevented deterioration; (8) Whether services such as financial assistance, housekeeper, vacations or summer camp for children have been rendered without evidence of movement.

Developing a classification of problems.—As noted before, no attempt was made in the development of the movement scale to differentiate between the types of problems coming to the caseworkers. Indeed, the difficulty or simplicity of the client's problem was specifically excluded as one of the considerations influencing the opinion of the judges as to whether movement had occurred. Hence this step in evaluative research was not dealt with in the development of the movement scale.

Standardizing the service that is offered.—No attempt was made in developing the movement scale to take into account the amount or type of service that was provided a client. The purpose of the study was simply to develop a measuring instrument, and the question of how much service produced what results was specifically excluded.

Methods of measuring change.—The movement scale is constructed of seven equal intervals ranging from -2 to represent the maximum degree of deterioration through -1, 0, $+1$, $+2$,

+3 to +4 for the maximum degree of forward movement or progress. Zero represents no *net* change, that is, it is used to indicate either that the client's status is essentially the same at the close of the case as it was at the opening or that progress in some respects is counterbalanced by deterioration in others. The positive numbers represent varying degrees of improvement or upward movement and the negative numbers, varying degrees of deterioration. Since there are four positive steps and only two negative ones, the scale lacks balance and was so designed for empirical reasons: The initial judges rated the maximum progress twice as great as the maximum deterioration found in the test cases.

For a rating of +4, the highest possible score for upward movement, evidence of progress in each of the four categories of criteria must be present in a marked degree. For a +3 score, each of the four types of evidence must also be present but in a lesser degree than for +4. The +2 rating does not require evidence of progress in all four categories, but it must be present in at least adaptive efficiency or disabling habits and conditions. For a rating of +1, the status of the client must clearly appear to be better in at least his environmental situation. Anchoring case illustrations are provided for the key steps —2, 0, +2, and +4 to facilitate judging the degree of movement by comparison of the change evident in the case being rated with the change depicted in the illustrative case summaries.

Initially, attempts were made to allow for only a single movement score for an entire case, but because it was found impracticable, this procedure was abandoned. As finally formulated, the movement scale calls for separate ratings for all individual clients in a case where (1) the scale is applicable, that is, where sufficient evidence is available to make possible a judgment rating on any individual in a case; and where (2) the scale is relevant, that is, where the movement judgment with respect to any individual in a case "has meaning as an index of the effectiveness of casework services." Both the applicability and relevance of the scale present difficult problems in applying the movement scale.

The manual on judging movement states that "in theory, applicability depends upon having sufficient evidence about the status of an individual's functioning and situation at two stages in time." However, this immediately raises the question as to what constitutes a sufficient body of evidence for application of the scale both to a case as a whole and to the individual clients in the case. No study was made of the degree of agreement of different judges on this question, although, on the basis of the field test of the movement scale, a minimum of five interviews on a case was selected as an objective criterion to indicate when sufficient evidence should be available for judgment. This criterion is admittedly a compromise which is somewhat arbitrary in order to achieve objectivity, but there is a question as to whether it would prove to be a feasible criterion in all agencies where the scale might be used. Furthermore, it does not solve the problem of the minimum evidence needed for determining the applicability of the scale to particular individuals in a case.

The results of the field test of the movement scale and other data from the Family Service Department of the Community Service Society indicate that this criterion of five interviews or more limits the applicability of the scale to somewhere between 10 percent and 26 percent of all cases and about 10 percent of all clients. On the other hand, this segment of the total case load receives approximately 90 percent of all casework interviews.

The relevance of the scale "involves the problem of when the movement rating for a given individual in a case may justifiably be considered to be an index of the effectiveness of the casework services provided for that person." The suggested criterion of relevance of the scale for particular individuals is whether or not the aim of the caseworker was improvement of that person or his situation in respect to any of the four criteria of movement. Thus, by definition, the scale is not relevant to all clients since there are clients who receive services, e.g., information on community resources, financial aid, and the like, where movement, as defined in this scale, is not a goal. On the other hand, it covers some individuals not ordinarily thought of as clients, since they are not seen or dealt with directly by the caseworker, but are affected indirectly by the service to or through others. To meet this latter difficulty, the procedure was suggested of having caseworkers formulate and state their goals in the record as soon as possible in a case to prevent or mitigate contamination of judgment on relevance at the close of the case. The goals stated near the beginning of a case can be compared with the four criteria of movement and decision made as to which individuals in the case the scale will ultimately be applied, rather than postponing comparison until the close of the case when knowledge of the outcome may influence this judgment. The reliability (degree·of agreement among independent judges) of the selection of particular individuals in a case for whom the scale is judged to be relevant was not tested in the development of the movement scale.

The objective in standardizing a judgment procedure is to achieve an acceptable degree of reliability (i.e., agreement) among independent judges. The reliability of the movement scale was checked in the field test by measuring the degree of agreement among 22 caseworkers of the Community Service Society trained in the use of the scale who independently judged the 38 test cases and by measuring the agreement between the judgments of these caseworkers on their own clients with those of an independent judge on those same clients. The average intercorrelation finally achieved among the judgments of these 22 workers on the individual clients in the 38 test cases was +.80 and the differences in the mean judgment of each set of judgments was within the range of a half-step interval on the movement scale.

Each of the 22 workers prepared special closing summaries on each of their cases of two or more client interviews closed between March 1, 1948, and July 31, 1948, in which evidence of movement in their clients was described. Each worker rated his own clients on the movement scale and all were rated by an independent judge on the basis of the closing summaries only. The correlation between the judgments of the caseworker on his own clients and those of the independent judge was +.80 and the difference in the mean judgment for all clients rated by the casework and by the independent judge was less than one-tenth of a step interval on the scale. It should be noted that the ratings of the independent judges were based on case summaries prepared by the workers who carried the case. It is quite easy to conceive of a worker slanting, unconsciously, a summary with the criteria of the movement scale in mind.

The procedures prescribed for use of the movement scale call for special training of each worker using the scale for the first time until his scores attain an acceptable degree of reliability as measured with the original test-case scores. Periodic testing of the reliability of the judgments of a caseworker routinely using the scale is also recommended.

Establishing causal relationships.—The movement scale does not, nor does it attempt to, establish any causal relationships between casework services and the progress or deterioration observed in the recipient of those services. It does not measure the results of casework as this phrase is ordinarily understood, but rather the change which occurs concurrently with the administering of casework services, regardless of whether that change is due to casework treatment or entirely independent of it.

Summary and over-all evaluation.—The development of the movement scale is among the most important evaluative studies in the social welfare profession. It represents the first major step toward the scientific evaluation of results in social casework, although admittedly it does not achieve the measurement of results necessarily produced by casework services. It has demonstrated that the judgment of caseworkers under specified conditions can attain a high degree of statistical reliability. By making use of the judgments of caseworkers, the movement scale is a relatively simple and inexpensive evaluative instrument to apply, which should make its routine use in agencies practicable. By its use of the movement concept, the movement scale not only adheres to current philosophy and practice in social casework, but also actually strengthens and emphasizes the importance of focus on the client, a basic tenet of casework theory. By specifying the major criteria and goals pursued by caseworkers, it should facilitate the teaching of casework and accelerate its improvement in practice. It opens up avenues for the improvement of the supervision and administration of casework services and for further research of possibly greater potential value than the movement scale itself.

Despite these actual and potential values, however, it is curious that the movement scale has received little actual acceptance or recognition from the profession after more than a year of its publication. It is not used by the Family Service Department of the Community Service Society under whose auspices it was developed at an enormous expenditure of money and time. Only one family casework agency—Family Service of Philadelphia—has adopted the movement scale as routine procedure. The Social Service Department of Washington University Clinic in St. Louis is the only other organization in the country which is presently making use of it. What is perhaps of even greater significance is the fact that relatively few caseworkers or teachers of casework have familiarized themselves with the movement scale despite the considerable publicity which it has been given.

There are acknowledged limitations of the movement scale. It has relevance only for those clients for whom casework goals involving movement have been set. The movement concept restricts the applicability of the scale solely to change in the client and/or his situation between the opening and closing of his case as determined by four specified categories of evidence. This excludes various types of casework services and the work of some specialized agencies. Furthermore, the scale is applicable only to those clients where sufficient evidence has accumulated to judge movement. This limits its use to cases with a minimum of five casework interviews, excluding some 75 percent to 90 percent of all intake cases and about 90 percent of all casework clients. However, those to which it can be applied receive about 80 percent of all casework services.

Insofar as the validity of the movement scale in measuring casework results is concerned, it represents but one step toward the goal, important as that step is. It leaves unanswered several major questions. To what extent does the movement scale measure the *actual* change in the client and/or his situation? Is the evidence discerned by the caseworker and recorded in his case record accurate and sufficiently complete to support valid judgments of change in the client? To what extent is movement caused by casework? To what extent do the results of casework persist after the service has been terminated? [2] What is the relation between movement and the quality of the casework service rendered? What is

[2] A companion study to the one described here is being conducted at the Institute of Welfare Research at the Community Service Society. Some 38 cases, in which adjustment of clients was rated as of the time of closing of the case, are being visited five or more years later to determine the extent to which the adjustment noted at the time of closing has changed.

the relation between movement and the kinds of problems the client has?

These are large questions. Answering them would require ambitious research undertakings and the far more active support and interest of the casework profession than it has hitherto demonstrated in achieving scientific methods of evaluating its own professional efforts.

CHANGING ATTITUDES THROUGH SOCIAL CONTACT, by Leon Festinger and Harold Kelly. Ann Arbor: Research Center for Group Dynamics, Institute for Social Research, University of Michigan, 1951.

Analysis of Methodology by Leon Festinger

Background of study.—This study arose from a general interest in satisfaction of residents in housing project communities. The first step in the study was a survey of a random sample of residents in a Federal Public Housing Project. The survey used intensive open-ended interviewing in an attempt to get some knowledge of the sources of satisfaction and dissatisfaction in the project, with respect to both physical and social conditions. The results of this initial survey provided the stimulus and the theoretical framework for the ensuing experiment. Those results may be summarized as follows:

1. There was a large incidence of feelings on the part of the residents that others in the project were "low class" people. Sixty-eight percent of those interviewed revealed such attitudes toward their neighbors.

2. As a result of these hostile attitudes toward their neighbors residents in the project tended to avoid contact with others in the project. They sometimes had a few selected acquaintants but they did not associate very much with the others.

3. The feeling was quite prevalent that people in the town looked down on the project residents, and as a result very few project people had friends in the town or belonged to clubs or other organizations.

From the data in the interviews hypotheses could be arrived at to explain the above syndrome of attitudes and social behavior which existed in the project. It seems that most residents in the project had come to live there not from choice but rather because it was impossible, at the time, to find any other place to live. They tended to have preconceived notions about the kinds of people who lived in government housing projects and felt it was "a step down" for them to live there. Most of them avoided getting to know the other people in the project, and, consequently, the attitudes with which they had come to the project persisted. Since they themselves looked down on the project and the others living in it, and were somewhat ashamed of living there, they naturally were convinced that outsiders felt the same way toward project residents.

It seemed plausible to assume from this analysis that if contact among the residents of the project could somehow be brought about, these attitudes, which had persisted because of the absence of such contact and experience, would start to change. Together with such attitude change we might expect to find changes in the pattern of social life in the project and changes in the relationship between project residents and townspeople. The attempt was made to bring about these contacts among project residents by involving them in various programs of community activities where they could work together and get to know each other. A number of professional community workers were employed to work with the residents of the project toward this goal.

With this brief outline of the background and purposes of the study in mind we will attempt to cover the five methodological points.

Establishing criteria against which success is to be measured.— Since the study could be said to have two purposes, a practical one and a theoretical one, the criteria for evaluating success can be looked at in two ways. From a practical point of view the purpose was to lessen the hostile attitudes toward neighbors among the project residents and, thereby, also to effect changes in the pattern of social life, in satisfaction with living in the community, and in relations with people outside the project.[1] The criteria

_____

[1] The criteria against which success is to be measured, for our purposes, are these practical goals which the community workers were seeking to realize through their activities.—Editor.

against which success would be measured become clear once these purposes are stated. We would have to, and did, obtain measures of attitudes toward neighbors and measures of satisfaction with living in the project; the number of friends and acquaintances in the project and the town; and information on membership in clubs, organizations, and the like.

The more theoretical objective of the study was to find out how such processes of change operate and the determinants of the time at which changes in attitudes do or do not occur. For this purpose we also wanted, and obtained, measures of extent of participation in the community activities, attitudes toward the community activities, and attitudes of outsiders toward the project. Success here would be measured in terms of whether or not we did discover some of the determinants of attitude change and whether or not we did obtain more understanding of the social processes involved.

Developing a classification of problems.—There was no classification of problems in this study. The initial survey, and the theoretical analysis on which the study was based, performed the function. What it amounted to was that one problem and its ramifications and consequences were taken as the focus of the study.[2] Many other kinds of problems undoubtedly existed, but these were ignored.

Standardizing the service that is offered.—There was no attempt in this study to standardize the service that was offered to the residents of the project. On the contrary, certain objectives were to be attained and the service the community workers offered was tailor-made to meet them. One of the objectives was to organize the community activities so that a maximum of working together and interpersonal contact among residents could be achieved.[3]

[2] The classification, or identification, of problems toward which the community workers directed their activity was sketched briefly by Mr. Festinger in the first part of this paper, namely: feelings that neighbors were "low class," absence of contact with other project residents, feelings of being looked down on by town residents, all of which resulted in lack of social contacts among project residents, and project residents and townspeople.— EDITOR.

[3] "Standardization of service offered" does not imply that a rigid set of activities, and these only, could be offered by the community workers. Standardiza-

Devising methods of measuring change.—Two data-collection procedures were used in the study, observation and interviewing. In order to get measures of participation in the community activities, the community workers wrote daily accounts in great detail of what they had done and what had taken place. These records included accounts of the meetings which took place, those who attended the meetings, persons contacted by the community workers, and the like. By coding and analyzing these records, measures of participation and changes in amount and character of participation in the activities could be obtained.

The main body of data was obtained by means of interviews. Since the investigators wanted progressive measures of change during the entire nine months of the experiment, surveys were done every two to two and a half months. These surveys were conducted on a random sample of 80 project residents and also on a random sample of 200 people living in the town, but geographically close to the project. In this way, by coding and analyzing the responses to various questions in the interview, several changes could be measured: in attitudes toward other residents and toward the project, in satisfaction with living in the project, in number of friends and acquaintances, in contact with townspeople, in attitudes of townspeople toward the project, and the like. Thus, since at the conclusion of the study there were four separate measurements, trends could be analyzed.

Establishing causal relationships.—Establishing causal relationships is most often an extremely difficult job in field studies or in field experiments. Generally the most one can do is to derive hypotheses about the causal relations involved without pinning them down conclusively. In the present study two things were

---

tion in this study could mean the provision of assistance to project residents in carrying out whatever activities served to bring them together and break down social distance, whether it was Saturday night square dances or a cooperative play group for preschool children. It is assumed that there was some standardization of the general approach of the community workers to project residents, so that some were not trying to impose a preconceived activity on one group, while others were trying to help a group plan and arrange activities of its own choosing. In other words, by virtue of the kind of personnel selected, there appears to have been a standardization of the *process* of working with the project residents, although there was no standardization of activities.—EDITOR.

done to try to make it likely that causal relationships might be established.

The study was set up as an experiment because this makes it easier to infer causality. If two things are simply observed to occur together it is generally impossible to know the dynamic relation between them. If, however, one variable, or set of variables, is changed at will and one observes that as these variables change there are other changes which result or take place, it makes the attribution of causality much safer. Even so, in a field experiment there are so many things which happen, in addition to the variables which are deliberately changed, that it is usually not completely conclusive that a certain change resulted from one designated variable.

As an additional safeguard it was decided to obtain many measurements rather than simply a "before and after" measure of change. In this way, if something serious happened to disturb things or to change conditions during the experiment, we would still be able to examine the data to see if the effects which were produced could be matched in time with various occurrences. This kind of analysis can lend more weight to hypotheses about causal relationships than would otherwise be the case.

AN EXPERIMENT IN THE PREVENTION OF DELINQUENCY, by Edwin Powers and Helen L. Witmer, New York: Columbia University Press, 1951.

Analysis of Methodology by Helen L. Witmer

Background of study.—This book is a report of the work and results of the Cambridge-Somerville Youth Study, a project set up and financed by Dr. Richard Cabot. Dr. Cabot maintained that many delinquent or potentially delinquent boys would develop into youths of steady and upright character if they were provided with the continued friendship and wise counsel of adults who were deeply interested in them and who could secure for them access to such community services as they required. In order to test this hypothesis Dr. Cabot established a service agency, the Cambridge-Somerville Youth Study, engaged a staff of counselors to render this kind of service, and selected from the public schools of two Massachusetts towns, Cambridge and Somerville, two series of boys, one of which was to receive the service and the other to act as a control group.[1]

According to the original plan the boys chosen for study were to be youngsters seven years old who seemed to be headed for delinquent careers. Since, however, teachers and others seemed unwilling or unable to identify such youths, the criterion for selection was changed to those "presenting difficulties" in school or elsewhere. The nature of the difficulties was undefined, with the result that the boys selected ranged from feeble-minded and neurologically disabled to frank delinquents. To these were added some "average" boys, so that the Study would not get a "bad name."

Pertinent data about the behavior, personality, make-up, and home situation of the boys chosen for study were secured by the counselors through questionnaires, psychological and medical tests, and interviews with parents, teachers, and the boys themselves. A "selection committee" was then set up which, by a complicated method of small-group matching, chose pairs of boys to constitute a study and a control series. Each series contained 325 boys, most of whom were nine to eleven years old by the time actual work with them got under way.

The service program lasted about seven years. During that time efforts were made by the counselors (who, for the most part, were not trained social workers) to keep in close touch with the boys and their families and to provide them with whatever kind of help seemed needed. The counselors varied considerably in their ways of working with the boys but, by and large, much emphasis was put on recreation, help with school difficulties and medical problems, and individual counseling of a big-brother variety. Most of the counselors were earnest, devoted, enthusiastic, and genuinely interested in the boys. Through their work, it

---

[1] "Control group" is the term used to describe the group of boys who were selected as comparable to the boys who received service from the Cambridge-Somerville Youth Study, but who actually received no service from the counselors. Their careers were followed to see how their adjustment compared with the adjustment of the boys who received the services of counselors.

seemed to us who were called in to evaluate the Study's results, Dr. Cabot's plan was adequately carried out.

When the service part of the program came to an end, outside research workers were asked to review the records and determine how successful the experiment had been. Their findings are reported in the second part of the volume, the first part being devoted to a description of the plan and the methods of work with the boys. The following analysis of the research refers chiefly to the study that was made after the service program ended.

Establishing criteria for success.—By the original research plan, success for the project as a whole (proof, that is, of the correctness of the hypothesis) would be demonstrated if a significantly greater proportion of the control boys than of the "treated" boys became delinquents. Such a comparison would have to take into account the nature and frequency of the offenses that occurred and the kinds of penalties imposed.

Dr. Cabot, however, also hoped and expected that the "treated" boys would excel the control boys in strength of character. He made no proposals as to how this was to be measured.

Classification of problems.—With "success" so classified (success for the boy in avoiding delinquency and in arriving at a satisfactory social adjustment; success for the counselor in being able to help the boy), the research workers wanted to be able to determine what kinds of boys were successful and what kinds of boys this type of service program could aid. This required a classification of the boys on the basis of "original adjustment," type of home (socially and emotionally considered), delinquency record, and so on.

With the exception of the objective aspects of the delinquency record, all classification systems were those of subjective description. The range of possibilities was determined through reading the records and through knowledge of the pertinent theory—for instance, that pertaining to parent-child relations. Rough, descriptive categories were then set up, cases representative of them determined, and all boys classified accordingly. In later, detailed analysis of the relations between results secured, services given, and home conditions and personality make-up, these categories served as guides to individual cases. In this process, too, they themselves were refined and the cases reclassified accordingly.

Standardization of service.—This step in evaluative research did not take place in the investigation since the evaluation of results followed upon the close of the service program. The fact that the service had not been standardized—that, in fact, the explicit plan was that each counselor should do as he thought best in the interests of friendship and that there should be little supervision of the usual casework variety—did prove an obstacle to research, as will be shown below.

Methods of measuring change.—The research workers who were called in to review the records accepted the original plan of Dr. Cabot and took as one of their measures of success the boys' court records. They also attempted to take into account the second objective of the Study, fostering strength of character, by setting up rough categories by which the individual boys' "social adjustment" at the beginning and at the end of the service program could be classified. In this classification system four grades of adjustment were recognized, ranging from good to poor as judged by behavior in relation to family, friends, school, and work. Rating of adjustment was by members of the research staff on the basis of information in the case records. Comparisons of beginning and terminal adjustments were made to determine whether boys had improved or declined one or more steps or had maintained their original standing.

While these measures, so called, of delinquency and social adjustment made the comparison of the study and control groups possible, they did not seem to the research workers really satisfactory, for they could give no hint as to the particular boys who had benefited and thus did not facilitate the answering of the question of most importance to professional social workers: under what circumstances and by what methods can "difficult" boys be aided?

An attempt was made, therefore, to determine case by case whether the boy had "probably," "possibly," or "definitely not" been aided by the counselors' services. In deciding in which of these three categories a "treated" boy should be placed, his behavior and his home and school adjustment at the time work with him started were examined. Note was then made of what the counselors did with and for him and his family and what concurrent changes took place in his life situation. On the basis of these facts a judgment was made as to whether there was a clear connection between the counselors' efforts and the improvement, if any, that had taken place in the boy's behavior.

As one means of checking on the validity of these judgments, a sample series of boys was interviewed by graduate students from Harvard, who had had no prior connection with the Study, and the boys' opinion of the value of the services ascertained. On the basis of these statements, the boys were again classified into groups ranging from those who thought the services were of real value to them to those who thought them useless.

Establishing causal relationships.—This, the most difficult problem in evaluative research, was handled in several ways.

First, according to the original plan set up by Dr. Cabot, causal relations were to have been established by the use of a control group. This seemed to us dubious reasoning, not so much for the usual reason given—that matching is impossible when personality and social relationships are under consideration—as that the "treatment" was diverse and unrelated, in many cases, to the boys' needs. It seemed to us that to give a great variety of services to a great variety of people, each practitioner doing what he thinks best without reference to any commonly held body of theory, is no more a scientific experiment—control group or no control group—than a medical one would be in which different kinds of medicine were given to patients suffering from different kinds of disorders by doctors who held different theories as to the causes of the illnesses.

If the study had shown that the "treated" boys did become delinquents much less frequently than the control boys we might have been beguiled into thinking that the value of this kind of service had been demonstrated. Perhaps that would have been a correct conclusion. Since it did not (the proportions of delinquents by any test was about the same in the two groups) we were forced to consider other ways of determining the connections between the services and results, for careful reading of the records made it clear that the counselors had been helpful in some cases.

As a second way of showing causal relationships, reliance was put on a comparison of boys rated as "clearly aided" with those rated as "possibly benefited" and those rated as "not helped," the cases in which the boy had never been in need of assistance being eliminated from consideration. It was reasoned that if the boys in these three categories were found to differ in ways that made good sense theoretically, the apparent difference in benefit derived was probably a real one. Such differences were found, on the basis of which conclusions were drawn as to the kinds of boys that can be aided by a program of this sort and the kinds of services such boys require.

As a third test—one which, in effect, was that of utilizing the control group data in a more refined way—the terminal social adjustment ratings of "treated" and control boys were compared, the value-of-service ratings being held constant. The numbers were small but statistically significant differences did appear. To cite only the extremes, in over half of the pairs of cases in which the treated boy was classified as having benefited, the treated boy's terminal adjustment rating was higher than that of his control "twin." Among the pairs in which the treated boy was classified as not having benefited, the reverse held true.

These various findings seemed to indicate that there was a causal connection between the services given and the apparent benefit to the boys. Not only did some boys change but the boys who changed differed from those who did not change both in the nature of their difficulties and in the kind of assistance they received. In spite of the very crude classifications, these differences stood out clearly. This seemed to the research workers to indicate that, while refinement of classification and improvement in method of testing results should be attempted, evaluation studies do not need to wait upon perfection of measuring devices. Much can be learned from careful, detached analysis along common-sense lines.

UNRAVELING JUVENILE DELINQUENCY, by Sheldon and Eleanor Glueck. New York: The Commonwealth Fund, 1950.

Analysis of Methodology by Alfred J. Kahn

This much discussed monograph [1] does not in a strict sense belong in any listing of evaluative research, and the pattern of analysis cannot strictly follow that proposed for evaluative research. The Gluecks have, in fact, turned their attention here from follow-up studies to a concern with causation of delinquency. In so doing, however, they have drawn on the lessons and hypotheses of their prior research as well as on the literature of the field. They have, too, met (and to a degree been overcome by) problems in classification and in research design as a whole which have broad relevance, particularly for the field of evaluative research.

The methodological problems are best introduced with a summary of the total procedure, as it appears on the publisher's book jacket:

"As a basis for the research, they matched five hundred persistently delinquent boys with five hundred truly non-delinquent boys in respect to ethnic derivation, age, intelligence quotient, and residence in underprivileged areas. The thousand boys were then classified anthropologically according to body types and were given medical and psychiatric examinations, intelligence and achievement tests, and the Rorschach Test. The family, school, and community background of each boy was thoroughly investigated by skilled social workers.

"In the interest of objectivity, each line of investigation was pursued independently; no one investigator had access to another's findings. As a result of their intensive multi-disciplinary approach, the authors arrive at a synthesis of the dynamic factors involved in juvenile delinquency.

"From among the factors found most markedly to differentiate delinquents from non-delinquents, the authors have developed prediction tables whereby they believe it feasible to differentiate

[1] See "Symposium" reviews by judges, lawyers, sociologists, psychiatrists, psychologists, and criminologists in *Federal Probation*, March, 1951, and *The Harvard Law Review*, April, 1951. See also the review by Philip Klein in *Social Work Journal*, April, 1951.

between potential juvenile offenders and non-offenders at early ages."

We shall not, except where it is relevant to a discussion of research design, repeat any of the considerable detail reported in the text about the above steps or about such very practical matters as the staff qualifications, sources of support for the study, procedures in obtaining permission, and matching techniques. It is important, however, to note the range of areas studied. The Gluecks move from data about the home and family life to appraisals of the interpersonal adjustments of the boys in their families, in school, and in the community. Following this, findings in relation to physical condition, health, and bodily constitution are analyzed. Then, the Bellevue-Wechsler comparisons are reported. Two chapters are based on Rorschach analysis, one devoted to "qualitative and dynamic aspects of intelligence" and another to character structure. Finally the evaluations by the psychiatrist are reviewed.

In each of the areas studied, the pattern of analysis remains the same:

1. Subjects are classified according to a large number of variables (size of household, culture conflict between American-born boy and foreign-born parents, age boy entered first grade, nature of functional deviations, methodical approach to problems—to cite, at randon, a few of the areas studied). The specific subcategories in each area are often those previously used by the Gluecks for classification in other studies; sometimes they represent modifications of such categories and, in some instances, such as the Rorschach analysis, they are new classification schemes.

2. The distributions for delinquents and non-delinquents are compared.

3. The differences found are subjected to statistical testing.

4. The significant differences are identified, discussed, and summarized at the end of each chapter. At the conclusion of the summary the authors separate so-called non-causal factors from the probably causal factors, and synthesize the latter into their "causal formula or law" (p. 281).

Without presenting detail we may indicate that the authors report, at the end of this process, that delinquents are distinguished from non-delinquents in five of the areas studied: (1) *physically* in being essentially mesomorphic; (2) *temperamentally* in being restlessly energetic; (3) *attitudinally* in being hostile, defiant, and adventurous; (4) *psychologically* in tending to direct and concrete expression rather than methodical and symbolic expression; (5) *socio-culturally* in deriving from homes which are to a lesser degree sources for emulation and construction of normal superegos.

The authors have found, too, that by employing weighting procedures with which they have previously experimented, it is possible to utilize factors most clearly differentiating delinquents from non-delinquents and to construct so-called prediction tables. They demonstrate how the use of such procedures properly categorizes most delinquents and non-delinquents in their groups although there is a range of error in misclassifications, varying with the factors utilized and the number of categories employed.

Hypotheses.—The social work field, which only too often meets studies that fail to consider the hypotheses deriving from all relevant sciences, can appreciate the decision of the Gluecks to deal not with a narrow hypothesis about delinquency but rather with a broad range of hypotheses on different levels. They do not wish to "ignore any promising leads to crime causation" and consequently utilize social work, psychiatry, psychology, sociology, medicine, and physical anthropology as collaborative disciplines in a broadly focused undertaking. One need hardly emphasize that a broad focus is the only means of advancing knowledge in this field beyond the mere statistical elaboration of the point of view of one group. (The sense in which this method has, however, resulted in creation of new problems will be discussed in the next section.)

As one example of the value of a broad view, we may mention the "under-the-roof" culture concept. Since the delinquents and non-delinquents were, on the surface at least, equated by neighborhood, it became legitimate to ask whether there were some environmental differences which were more subtle and which differentiated the groups. In exploring this lead, the Gluecks have clarified some of the factors that distinguish the families and homes which breed delinquency and those which do not, although both groups of homes are in what superficially seem like similar environments. In assembling these data, the Gluecks have shown, by implication, why so many sociological investigations which never got "under-the-roof" were doomed to superficiality just as they have in other parts of the study shown the limitations of a purely psychiatric study of delinquency causation.

Despite recognition that the very phenomenon they wish to explain, delinquency, is really a phenomenon with many subtypes, the Gluecks do nothing about this. The problems created by such failure are described in the final section.

Assemblying data.—The various phases of this procedure have apparently been executed with considerable care.

Great effort has gone into the development of elaborate case files on 1,000 boys, the verification of all important data, and the obtaining of all available social agency, institution, and school reports. Tests were carefully administered and scored. The matching procedure is elaborate but necessary in the light of the authors' conception of the problem. The one case history available to me for review suggests systematic work by all team members. One might also mention at random such other "positives" as the fact that all anthropometric indices were repeated after an interval to check reliability. The psychologist who analyzed the Rorchachs did not know which records were those of delinquents. There is every evidence that the home interviews were quite skillful. A good deal of ingenuity went into developing an administrative structure to assure systematic study of each case and appropriate follow-up of missing data. There was great care too in case coding, card punching, and tabulation. Statistical results are clearly presented and there has been some understanding (p. 76) that "a statistically significant difference is not always a significant one."

The choice of large numbers of cases for each of the groups has served to guarantee a sufficient number of cases in each subcategory of analysis. It is thus possible to avoid the dilemmas of many studies based on too few cases.

What is more, data and analyses are so presented as to enable the reader to separate at all times data, conclusions, inferences, and opinions about significance. This is a reasonable expectation in a scientific monograph, but it represents a standard frequently violated.

The Gluecks have not, however, faced possible major sources of error in the data. The home interviews were conducted by individuals who, of necessity, knew which were and which were not families from which delinquents derived. It is quite possible (pp. 108 ff.) that the family life data are "contaminated" by this knowledge. What is more, we must note that much of the attitude data (affection of mother for boy, emotional ties of boy to father, etc.) is based on attitudes identified after the boy was a known delinquent, with all the consequences that holds for family relationships. This material is nonetheless used to explain *causation*.

The sample and the logic of group matching.—It was decided (and the choice was indeed necessary in light of current hypotheses) to keep certain factors constant in making the comparisons between the delinquent and non-delinquent groups. The delinquents and non-delinquents were matched in respect to ethnic derivation, age, I.Q., and area of residence. The authors recognize and state (p. 14) that this means that the results cannot throw light on the very factors which have been controlled. However, this very important fact is not considered in the later development of the "law" of delinquency causation. The fault does not lie in the initial matching, since some factors had to be controlled, but rather in the failure to note that one cannot formulate a "law" without other study in which these factors would become variables.

This problem may be described in still another way. When one arrives at a finding in regard to a sample, the conclusion may be said to apply only to the universe of which the sample is a representative segment. This also holds for findings based on a comparison of matched samples, as in the present instance. It may be true, as the authors state, that most delinquents come from economically underprivileged areas. They are, however, reporting on delinquency, not on *some* or most delinquents, and they fail in their conclusions to recall the basis of case matching.[2]

The Gluecks, too, in attempting to apply their findings to all delinquents, have failed to face the well-known fact that institutionalized offenders (all their delinquent cases) are in no sense representative of all delinquents.

[2] Ernest W. Burgess, in "Symposium," *Federal Probation* (March, 1951), goes further and states that the Gluecks have allowed too much variation in the matching.

Establishing causal relationships.—The values of assuring an eclectic approach so that all relevant levels of inquiry will be pursued have been stated above. The problems deriving from such an approach deserve elaboration.

1. It is quite obvious that a broadly eclectic approach such as is here undertaken cannot do more than to list, in each of the levels of inquiry undertaken, all factors considered as possibly differentiating the delinquent from the non-delinquent and to determine which factors do and which do not truly differentiate. What is more, one is limited as to which areas of the past one can reconstruct because of (p. 41) "limitations in recorded data and in the memories of those from whom the information must necessarily be derived." It is "difficult to secure any valid qualitative data, such as the emotional atmosphere surrounding past and even current situations . . ." (p. 41).

The result tends to be a purely empirical procedure which may be brilliant in its ingenuity and careful in its method but which is nonetheless quite opportunistic. Eventually, such a study can do no more than study factors which readily lend themselves to study and then list, from among those factors, those which do differentiate the two groups and those which do not. There are no areas seen as basic minimums in investigation.

The extent to which this is to be regarded as a serious problem in this study varies with the view of what it is that the authors believe they are doing. If they believe (p. 281) that they are establishing a scientific *law*, however temporary, one must attack and criticize the view vigorously. If, on the other hand, the intention is (p. 55) "establishing the gross differences between delinquents and non-delinquents in order eventually to narrow the field of more intensive exploration of crime causation" one's evaluation changes.

A scientific law can be established only on the basis of an experimental study in which a clear hypothesis is presented and in which the experiment is designed to see whether the hypothesis is nullified. This is not the situation in the present volume. The authors have identified areas which are considered by various investigators, representing different disciplines, as having data to contribute. Using data which seemed relevant and which were accessible within the limits of the time, staff, and design, they have attempted to identify differentiating factors. They have then attempted to weave these factors into a pattern of explanation.

It is Ernest Schachtel who states in Appendix E what I believe to be the character of this study. He writes: ". . . this study is not experimental but explorative and is not intended to prove or disprove any preconceived hypothesis, but to serve as a basis for developing hypotheses." The Gluecks apparently agree with this statement since they permit its publication, yet one cannot help but feel that they are somehow convinced that more has been accomplished.

It becomes necessary to observe, once this clarification is established, that the Gluecks are only *partially* successful in the more modest undertaking of moving from a listing of factors to the formulation of a hypothesis. This point can be better developed only after the introduction of several added considerations.

2. One must note particularly, in examining the comparisons of the two groups, that even though differences which are statistically significant are identified, we are often dealing with factors which may characterize a minority of each group or a majority in both groups. In other instances, the difference may be significant but small. Thus, more delinquents than non-delinquents come from homes in which there are more than two occupants per bedroom (Table VIII-7) but this condition is true in only 32.6 percent of the homes of the delinquents and 24.8 percent of the control group. More non-delinquents are reported (Table VIII-8) as coming from normally neat and clean homes, but the fact remains that 48.7 percent of the delinquents come from such homes. It may be true (Table X-6) that more delinquents than non-delinquents come from homes with poor conduct standards, but the fact remains that the majority of non-delinquents (54 percent) come from such homes. The mean family size of the delinquents' families is significantly larger than that of the non-delinquents, but, again, the actual difference (p. 119) is small. One could cite many other tables to illustrate these same points. Many of the Rorschach differences (example, p. 218) are often of an order involving a minority of both groups.

Occasionally, too (p. 89), the authors seem to ignore the fact that their testing shows no statistical significance for obtained differences, and they proceed to elaborate on tables in the text. They might well counter that where differences are small or not significant statistically, they are considered if they are "in one direction." This is an important argument and provides leads useful in hypothesis construction if one recognizes that there are probably important intervening variables not yet identified. The practice is not defensible if one intends merely to add factors at the end and present a "sum."

3. The temptation is generally avoided but the authors at several points introduce *ad hoc* explanations in the midst of their presentation of data. Thus (p. 125) since only half as many fathers of the delinquents as of the non-delinquents evidenced warmth, sympathy, and affection toward their boys, the authors note that "the growing child may seek substitute anti-social satisfactions in companionship with delinquent children, or he may pass through a stage of grave insecurity, frustration, and resentment, with resultant psychoneurotic symptoms." Now, all of this may be correct and this is surely a legitimate hypothesis to pose on the basis of the data—but it is vital that one separate the data from this hypothesis and recognize that this is not yet a finding.

An even more complex difficulty is yet to be reported—one which is either not recognized by the Gluecks or, if recognized, is superficially solved. The problem arises, in comparing delinquents with non-delinquents, as to how one decides which are comparisons made to identify possible causal factors and which comparisons do no more than identify differences incidental to or following from the delinquency and institutionalization. This may be illustrated with reference to Chapter XII, "The Boy in the School." Without reviewing detail, one might state that in general, the delinquents reveal maladaptation to the codes of school in greater numbers than do the non-delinquents (see, for example, pp. 143, 144, 148, 154). This finding does not settle the question of whether the school is a "cause" or whether the school difficulty is just another aspect of the delinquency. Some aspects of this difficulty are readily solved since one can, for instance, remind the authors (p. 148) that of course non-delinquents are not persistent truants since persistent truancy would make them delinquents. Furthermore, events which occur in school *after* the first reported delinquencies can be eliminated as possible causes of such delinquencies. Most of the factors described in this and other chapters cannot be dealt with in this manner, however.

4. There is a point in research of this kind that no multiplication of gadgets, tools, or careful procedure can substitute for clarity about research design and about what one means in discussing "causal" relationships. The authors are able, quite usefully (pp. 272–273), to rule out factors which do not differentiate delinquents and non-delinquents, but they do not critically appraise what remains. How is one to decide whether the presence of mesomorphy is a cause of delinquency or an incidental characteristic of institutionalized delinquents? Is "adventurousness" a cause, or is it part of a configuration which describes the pattern we call delinquency?

There is no formal way to answer these questions. They point up a limitation which dominates throughout a volume in which no attempt is made to differentiate *description* and *cause*. This is inevitable since the authors do not discuss at any point, or seem to face, what they will mean by cause. Of the several possible approaches, they seem to follow none to their logical and methodological implications.

The result is inevitable. We have at the end (as indicated) not a scientific law but rather the very beginnings of a crude hypothesis. What is more, the hypothesis seems to deal not with how delinquency is *caused* but rather with what it *is*. The Gluecks seem at some points to recognize that they are not at the state of causal knowledge but of "reflections upon materials" (p. 281), yet they do not at any point acknowledge the final failure to differentiate the descriptive and characteristic from the causal.

5. Scientific study aims at prediction and control, and the Gluecks have widely advertised this as well as previous works as contributions to prediction. Theoretically, a predictive tool can be developed in a completely empirical procedure, so that the lack of clarity about causation should not, necessarily, nullify

the prediction tables. There is, however, by now a broad range of experience with prediction instruments and a good deal of clarity about the logic of prediction.[3] This experience and these logical considerations suggest the following as a partial critique of the prediction tables: [4]

a) The predictive factors employed are *not* here established as being available at the time a child enters school. The Gluecks feel such data could be available, but the fact remains that the examinations, tests, and social studies here reported were made for older children. A predictive instrument cannot be said to exist until it is developed and employed in the manner in which it is meant to be used ultimately.

b) It is a basic rule in developing prediction instruments that they must be validated on a new group, not the group on which they have been developed, to eliminate the possibility that data idiosyncracies determine the instrument. The Gluecks report the need for "experimental application" but then proceed (p. 269) to "oversell" the instrument in its current state.

c) An instrument of prediction may be used only with a group similar to the one for which it was standardized. The Gluecks do not recall the limitations concerning ethnic derivation, age, I.Q., and residence in presenting this material for use.

d) The fourth objection has to do not with method but with values. One must ask whether we need a means of identifying potential *delinquents* at an early age, or rather vulnerable *children* likely to develop a variety of forms of disturbance and maladjustment and in need of help. A strong case can be made for attempting to screen out a broader group, particularly since the Gluecks' non-delinquents show many evidences of needing help.

e) The Gluecks recognize but have not at all handled the issue of developing an instrument which is not too complex or expensive for use. Their current one may be so characterized.

f) It is necessary to test the degree of error involved in applying this instrument as compared with the error of far simpler procedures.

[3] Paul Horst, *The Prediction of Personal Adjustment* (Social Science Research Council, 1941).
[4] There are more detailed discussions in the "Symposium" referred to in n. 1 above.

Research design and logic.—The Gluecks have labored in a complex area and have met difficult problems of method and of analysis. They have drawn upon available procedures, have brought their own rich background of experience, have had the advice of qualified consultants, and the help of competent staff. As a result, the methodological *details* of the study are in many ways admirable. This does not, however, make up for the crucial deficiencies in the formulation of the problem, the definition of the phenomenon studied, and the analysis of the findings.

The present study has already ruled out some variables as not being fruitful areas of study. It has, furthermore, made available raw material for hypothesis construction, although this material requires careful analysis to sort out what is considered "causal" and what is seen as characteristic description of the personality and background of the delinquent child. But more than this is required in future work; some of the needs are stated or implied in the text, others are missed.

There must be clarity, first, about the concept of "cause." Are the authors seeking consistent high-order correlations, or do they wish to be able to trace a process and show the detailed dynamics behind an act? Do they mean "cause" in an absolute, ultimate sense, or are they answering more modest questions—such as, in what sense does the parent-child-relationship contribute to delinquency; in what sense and manner does school experience contribute to or prevent delinquency, etc.? Are they perhaps interested in the discovery of a series of intervening variables which mathematically account for relationships between other variables?

At the same time as there is clarification of "cause," there must be more precise delimitation of the phenomena studied, delinquency. The Gluecks know (p. 13) and Schachtel states very clearly (p. 379) that delinquency is neither a psychiatric nor a psychological concept. There is good reason to believe (p. 275) "that the delinquent group is a composite of several sub-types." The use of the social definition here employed represents the attempt to study the phenomenon as defined by institutions working with delinquents. However, the very grouping of many sub-types into the group studied, as one searches for causation, may blur possibly profitable leads. If, instead, one might regard this volume, not as a tentative answer but rather as a first step in the study of the delinquency phenomenon, next steps would be clear. Following additional studies of the phenomenon of delinquency itself, it would be possible to identify and isolate homogeneous classes of so-called delinquents and then to study causation within each class. The data in this volume tend to suggest that the basis for such categorization might well be such aspects of individual personality as attitude toward authority (see Schachtel's suggestion on p. 217) or perhaps one's constitutional make-up and reaction patterns.

The Gluecks see the study as leading ultimately to both further study of causation (intercorrelation of factors, etc.) and to evaluative studies (follow-up studies and behavior during treatment). They mean to do more, too, with the predictive instruments. In the latter regard, one must stress particularly that they have thus far predicted only *backward* and must ultimately attempt *forward* prediction to avoid idiosyncracies of the one group studied. More important, however, is the need to emphasize that any study of causation of a phenomenon requires far stricter definition of the phenomenon, far greater clarity about cause, and, therefore, far more attention to the logic of research design.

INDEX

Adult offenders: expenditures for services to, through state governmental departments in Michigan (1950), 18(*tab.*); number of social workers in Michigan (1948) engaged in social work with, 14(*tab.*)

Aged, the: expenditures in Michigan (1950) for services to, 17(*tab.*); financial assistance to, 16; number served in institutions in Detroit (1950), 21(*tab.*)

Aid to dependent children, number of recipients in Michigan (1950), 20

Andrews, Emerson, quoted, 117

Applied research, 76, 98; *see also* Research in social work

Baker Child Guidance Center (Boston), 89

Basic research, 76; *see also* Research in social work

Blenkner, Margaret, 32, 141*n*

Blind, the: financial assistance to, 16; number of recipients of aid in Michigan (1950), 20

Boston, Judge Baker Child Guidance Clinic in, 89

Bronner, Augusta F., 89

Bureau of Applied Social Research (Columbia University), 98

Cabot, Richard, 155

Cambridge (Mass.), youth study, 60, 67-68, 155-60

Cambridge-Somerville Youth Study, 60, 67-68, 155-60

Cartwright, Dorwin, quoted, 92

Categorical assistance, 20

Changing Attitudes through Social Contact (Festinger and Kelly), 50*n*, 151-55

Chase, Stuart: cited, 31, 79; quoted, 23

Chein, Isidor, cited, 42

Children's Bureau of the Federal Security Agency, 120

Children Who Hate (Redl), 103*n*

Child welfare: conferences on, 24-43; 125-40; expenditures in Michigan (1950) for, 17(*tab.*); expenditures through state governmental departments in Michigan (1950) for, 18(*tab.*); number of social workers in Michigan (1948) in, 14(*tab.*); problems in, 24

Child Welfare League of America, 50

"Clinical fallacy," 66-67

Clinics, *see* under specific type, e.g., Mental hygiene clinics

Columbia University Bureau of Applied Social Research, 98

Community chests: expenditures by voluntary agencies affiliated with, 17; number in Michigan, 13

Community organization work, number of social workers in Michigan (1948) in, 14(*tab.*)

Community planning, expenditures in Michigan (1950) for, 17(*tab.*)

Community services, evaluative study of, 50, 151-55

Community Service Society (New York City), 52-53, 62, 89, 141

Conant, James Bryant, quoted, 81-82

"Conceptual frameworks," 57

Conference of Charities and Corrections, 74

Conference on Social Services for Children (Michigan, 1951), 24-43, 125-40

Contract research, 93-94, 100; *see also* Research in social work